1 MONTH OF
FREE
READING

at

www.ForgottenBooks.com

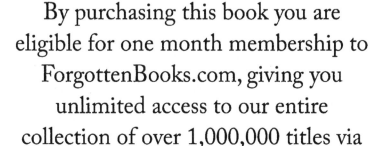

By purchasing this book you are
eligible for one month membership to
ForgottenBooks.com, giving you
unlimited access to our entire
collection of over 1,000,000 titles via
our web site and mobile apps.

To claim your free month visit:

www.forgottenbooks.com/free901798

ISBN 978-0-266-86752-4
PIBN 10901798

ANNUAL REPORT

OF THE

OFFICERS

OF THE

TOWN OF

TUFTONBORO

N. H.

For The Fiscal Year
Ending January 31

1935

EARL R. DALE
PRINTING OFFICE
EAST WOLFEBORO N. H.

LIST OF TOWN OFFICERS FOR 1934

Representative to General Court
FRANK A. HILLIARD

Town Clerk
MARION L. HORNER

Selectmen
FORREST W. HODGDON   EDWIN B. EDGERLY
FRANK S. BENNETT

Tax Collector
AUSBREY N. DOW

Treasurer
M. ETHEL BENNETT

Constable
HENRY F. HAYES

Health Officer
HENRY F. HAYES

Police Officers
CHARLES E. HERSEY   MILTON LORD

Auditors
MARY J. BLAKE   JOHN E. BENNETT

Supervisors of Check List
EDWIN C. HERSEY   HARRY L. DAVIS
MILTON LORD

Road Agent
DELMA McINTIRE

Trustees of Trust Funds
EDWIN C. HERSEY   MARY J. BLAKE
RALPH V. BENNETT

Library Trustees
HATTIE HERSEY   EDA M. DAVIS
GEORGE S. HORNER

Warrant for the Annual Town Meeting, March 12, 1935

THE STATE OF NEW HAMPSHIRE

To the inhabitants of the town of Tuftonboro in the (L. S.) *County of Carroll in said State, qualified to vote in Town Affairs:*

You are hereby notified to meet at the Town Hall in said Tuftonboro on Tuesday, the twelfth (12) day of March next, at nine of the clock in the forenoon, to act upon the following subjects:

1. To choose all necessary Town Officers for the year ensuing.

2. To raise such sums of money as may be necessary to defray town charges for the ensuing year and make appropriation of the same.

3. To see if the Town will accept State Aid for construction of the class 2 road, known as the Mountain Road, and raise and appropriate or set aside for said purpose, the sum of $1,768. or will accept State Aid for construction of class 5 roads, and raise and appropriate, or set aside for said purpose, the sum of $343.04.

4. To see if the Town will vote to raise and appropriate the sum of $2,000. for improvements and tar on Tuftonboro Neck and Wawbeek Roads.

5. To see if the town will vote to raise and appropriate the sum of $500. for legal expenses incurred on Lake Road, and Islands.

6. To see if the town will vote to raise and appropriate the sum of $100. for Huggins Hospital.

7. To see if the town will vote to authorize the Selectmen to borrow money in anticipation of taxes to be levied for the year 1935.

8. To see if the town will vote to raise and appropriate the sum of $2,000. for the payment of a note due February 1, 1936.

9. To see if the town will vote to install electricity in the Town Hall, and raise and appropriate money for the same.

10. To see if the town will vote to raise the sum of $300. to remove the ledge at Ledge Hill, agreeable to petition signed by Herbert Ayers and others.

11. To see if the town will vote to raise $1,500. to rebuild the public wharf at Melvin Village, and to appropriate money for the same, agreeable to petition signed by Ralph W. Drucker and others.

12. To see if the people of Tuftonboro will request the Seleetmen to petition the head of the Highway Commission to see if they will remove the triangle plot, and private signs at the intersection of the State Road and Tuftonboro Neck Road, agreeable to petition, signed by Carl B. Johnson and others.

13. To see what sum of money the town will raise and appropriate to build a public wharf at the site of the old Union Wharf at the Lower Bay; agreeable to petition signed by Carroll Lamprey and others.

14. To see if the town will vote to put on two or more crews to run the snow plows and tractor at Tuftonboro Corner, agreeable to petition signed by Myron Haley and others.

15. To see if the Town will vote to accept the provisions of the Municipal Budget Act.

16. To see if the town will vote to raise and appropriate the sum of $400. for the suppression of white Pine Blister Rust.

17. To transact any other business that may legally come before said meeting.

Given under our hands and seal, this twenty-fifth day of February, in the year of our Lord nineteen hundred and thirty-five.

FORREST W. HODGDON	Selectmen
EDWIN B. EDGERLY	of
FRANK S. BENNETT	Tuftonboro

A true copy of Warrant—Attest:

FORREST W. HODGDON	Selectmen
EDWIN B. EDGERLY	of
FRANK S. BENNETT	Tuftonboro

Budget of the Town of Tuftonboro, N.

Estimates of Revenue and Expenditures for the Ensuing Yea February 1, 1935, to January 31, 1936, Compared with Actu Revenue and Expenditures of the Previous Year February 1, 193 to January 31, 1935.

Sources of Revenu

	Actual Revenue Previous Year 1934	Estimated Revenue Ensuing Year 1935	Increase	Decrease
From State:				
Insurance Tax	$308 00	$308 00		
Savings Bank Tax	747 26	700 00		
E. R. U.	2 240 70			
Interest and Dividend Tax	1 094 69	1 000 00		
Bounties		73 40		
From Local Sources Except Taxes:				
Interest Received on Taxes and Deposits	22 36	20 00		
Income of Departments: Highways etc.	236 75	100 00		
Material	27 32			
Dog Licenses	210 00	210 00		
Gift	25 00	25 00		
Refunds	22 24			
From Poll Taxes:				
Poll Taxes	750 00	750 00		
From Other Taxes Except Property Taxes:				
National Bank Stock	2 00	2 00		
Filing Fees	8 00			
Motor Vehicle Permit Fees	706 93	700 00		
Anticipation of Taxes	2 000 00	2 000 00		

Purposes of Expenditu

	Actual Expenditures Previous Year 1934	Estimated Expenditures Ensuing Year 1935	Increase
General Government:			
Town Officers' Salaries	$774 00	$900 00	
Town Officers' Expenses	527 02	500 00	
Care and Supplies for Town Hall	105 00	25 00	
Protection of Persons and Property:			
Insurance	330 23	250 00	
Police Department	53 75	50 00	
Fire Department	228 66	200 00	
Bounties	24 00		
Health:			
Health Department, Including Hospitals	100 00	100 00	
Vital Statistics	4 75	5 00	
Highways and Bridges:			
Town Maintenance	3 401 17	3 000 00	
Bushes	399 83	400 00	
General Expense of Highway Dept.	1 382 44	1 500 00	
Libraries:			
Libraries	81 50	81 50	
Charities:			
Town Poor	204 32	300 00	
Other Expenditures:			
Legal Expenses	147 75	500 00	
Patriotic Purposes:			
Memorial Day and Other Celebrations	25 00	25 00	
Interest:			
On Temporary Loans	25 00	25 00	
On Long Term Notes	338 33	300 00	
Outlay For New Construction and Permanent Improvements:			
E. R. U.	2 240 70		
Town Construction			
Tuftonboro Neck and Wawbeek	965 05	2 000 00	
State Aid Const., State's Contribution	1 744 90	1 768 00	
" " " Town's Contribution	1 744 90	1 768 00	
New Equipment	710 60		
Indebtedness:			
Long Term Notes	2 000 00	2 000 00	
Payments to Other Governmental Divisions:			
State Taxes	2 379 00	2 379 00	
County Taxes	4 633 50	4 633 50	
Payments to School Districts	7 228 75	7 000 00	

Summary of Inventory

Land and Buildings		$1 064 965 00
No. of Acres	21 553	
Electric Plants		29 000 00
Horses	58	3 350 00
Asses	2	100 00
Oxen	9	500 00
Cows	206	6 436 00
Neat Stock	52	1 510 00
Fowl	1 898	1 134 25
Boats and Launches	75	60 500 00
Wood and Lumber		2 992 00
Gasolene Pumps and Tanks	38	2 700 00
Stock in Trade		5 825 00
Mills and Machinery		500 00
		$1 179 512 25

Polls 375 @ $2.00 $750.00

Rate of Taxation $20.00 per thousand

Soldier Exemptions $8,700.00

List of Appropriations

Town Officers' Salaries	$775 00
Town Officers' Expenses	400 00
Town Hall Expenses	25 00
Police Department	50 00
Fire Department	200 00
Insurance	175 00
Huggins Hospital	100 00
Town Maintenance	3 000 00
Bushes	400 00
General Highway Department Expenses	1 000 00
Painting Town Hall	150 00
Libraries	81 50
Town Poor	300 00

Memorial Day	$25 00
Interest	475 00
Tar for Tuftonboro Neck and Wawbeek	1 000 00
State Aid Construction	1 740 00
Long Term Note	2 000 00
Forest Fire Pumps	50 00
Snow Plows	600 00
County Tax	4 633 50
State Tax	2 379 00
Schools	7 040 35
	$26 599 35

Assets

Cash on hand	$402 52
Due from State, hedgehog bounties	73 40
" " " blister rust	7 00
" " " balance of E. R. U.	20 70
" " " " " S. A. C.	1 03
" " Ralph Horn, 2 days power shovel	50 00
" " Town of Wolfeboro, breaking roads	20 00
" " A. N. Dow, collector,	
uncollected 1934 taxes	431 35
Total	$1 006 00

Liabilities

Notes due Wolfeboro National Bank

Date of Note	Due	Amount
Apr. 18, 1932	Feb. 1, 1936	$2 000 00
Feb. 1, 1935	Feb. 1, 1937	2 000 00
Note due W. W. Thomas		500 00
" " " " " guardian of		
	Hattie McIntire	1 500 00
	Total liabilities	$6 000 00
	Total assets	1 006 00
	Net debt	$4 994 00

Town Clerk's Report

Receipts

1934 Automobile permits No. 137,982 - 138,097 inc.				$315	57
1935 Automobile permits No. 140,351 - 140,480 inc.				391	36
85 Dog licenses					
19 @ $5 00			$95 00		
66 @ 2 00			132 00		
				$227	00
Filing fees				8	00
				$941	93

Payments

1934

Mar.	3	John A. Edgerly, treasurer, auto permits	$7	31
Apr.	3	M. Ethel Bennett, " " "	48	07
May	5	" " " " " "	46	51
June	5	" " " " "	66	52
July	2	" " " " " "	20	57
Aug.	2	" " " " " "	45	20
	2	" " filing fees	8	00
Oct.	5	" " " auto permits	25	99
Nov.	10	" " " " "	8	62
Dec.	6	" " " " "	109	94
1935				
Jan.	7	" " " " " "	278	25
	31	" " " " " "	49	95
	31	" " " " dog licenses	210	00
	31	" Marion L. Horner, clerk's fees for issuing dog licenses	17	00
			$941	93

Tax Collector's Report

Dr.

Property tax warrant	$23 590 25
Poll tax warrant	736 00
Interest on taxes	22 36
Additional taxes picked up	14 00
Total liabilities	$24 362 61

Cr.

June 12	Paid Ethel Bennett, town treasurer	$2 800 00
July 12	" " " " "	5 300 00
Sept. 1	" " "	2 100 00
Oct. 31	" " "	4 100 00
Dec. 12	" " "	4 000 00
Jan. 10	" " "	3 600 00
31	" " "	1 667 76
Feb. 7	" " " "	363 50
Jane Burleigh,	uncollected tax	19 00
Wyatt D. Cheney,	" "	15 80
Bertha Haley,		70 00
Charles W. Haley,		20 70
Forrest Hersey,		. 50
George F. Howe,		16 00
Jonathan Hodgdon, Est.,		30 00
Peter Kidd,		3 00
Robert Page,		24 00
John F. Piper,		11 79
Clyde Gerald,		14 00
George Straw,		20 40

Chester Thomas,	uncollected tax		$34 30
Florence I. Woodmancy,	"	"	13 86
Mr. Anderson,			2 00
Eula Durland,			20 00
E. M. Sams,			22 00
Fred A. Wiggin,	"	"	54 00
Lillian Cheney,	"	poll tax	2 00
Geo. "		" "	2 00
Mattie "	"	" "	2 00
Wyatt "			2 00
Harold Edwards,			2 00
Bertha Haley,			2 00
Chas. W. Haley,			2 00
Dora Haley,			2 00
* Margaret Hilliard,	"		2 00
* Louis "			2 00
Forest Hersey,		" "	2 00
Lizzie "			2 00
Angie Kane,			2 00
Jennie Robbins,		" "	2 00
Clarence Staples,			2 00
Elsie "			2 00
Chester Thomas,	"	" "	2 00
Effie "			2 00
Ethel Morrill,		" "	2 00
Elizabeth Buswell,			2 00

$24 362 61

* Paid

Treasurer's Report, Summary
February 1, 1934, to February 1, 1935
Receipts

Cash on hand Feb. 1, 1934	$637 25
A. N. Dow, Collector, Taxes	24 137 99
" " " I. D. Barber 1933 Tax and Interest	721 73
State of New Hampshire, E. R. U.	2 240 70
" " " " Insurance tax	3 08
" " " " Savings Bank tax	747 26
Interest and Dividends	1 094 69
Rental of town plow	27 00
" " " " " " " tractor	59 50
Town of Ossipee, rental of town plow and tractor	150 25
Andrew Goldman, 1933 liability	20 00
Camp Belknap, gift	25 00
Otis Hersey, 1933 uncancelled check	2 24
Delma McIntire, road building material sold to State	15 68
" " culvert on Spear Road	11 64
New Public National Bank of Rochester, National Bank stock tax	2 00
Wolfeboro National Bank, note	2 000 00
Town Clerk, Auto permits	706 93
" " Dog licenses	210 00
" " Filing fees	8 00
Total	$32 820 94

Expenditures

Orders from Selectmen	$32 418 42
Balance on hand, Jan. 31, 1935	402 52
	$32 820 94

M. ETHEL BENNETT,
Treasurer.

Summary of Payments

Town Officers' Salaries	$774 00
Town Officers' Expenses	527 02
Town Hall Expenses	105 00
Police Department	53 75
Fire Department	228 66
Insurance	330 23
Bounties	24 00
Chapman School Building	1 00
Huggins Hospital	100 00
Vital Statistics	4 75
Town Maintenance	3 401 17
Bushes	399 83
General Expenses of Highway Department	1 382 44
New Equipment	710 60
Libraries	81 50
Town poor	204 32
Patriotic Purposes	25 00
Interest	363 33
Discounts and Abatements	362 17
Legal Expenses	147 75
Town Construction	965 05
State Aid Construction	1 744 90
Emergency Relief Unemployment	2 240 70
Temporary Loans	2 000 00
Long Term Note	2 000 00
County Tax	4 633 50
State Tax	2 379 00
Schools	7 228 75
	$32 418 42

General Government

Town Officers' Salaries

Dec.	4	A. L. Ridlon, 3 days ballot clerk	$10 50
	17	Harry L. Davis, services as supervisor	24 00
	20	Frank S. Bennett, " in part as selectman	25 00
1935			
Jan.	31	Edwin C. Hersey, services as supervisor	24 00
	31	Thomas H. Blaisdell, " " ballot clerk	10 50
	31	Eda M. Davis, " " " "	10 50
	31	Alice Goodrich, " " " "	10 50
	31	Marion L. Horner, " " town clerk	40 00
	31	John A. Edgerly, " " moderator	15 00
	31	M. Ethel Bennett, " " treasurer	85 00
	31	Forrest W. Hodgdon, " " selectman and overseer of poor	110 00
	31	E. B. Edgerly, services as selectman	100 00
	31	Frank S. Bennett, " " " balance	75 00
	31	A. N. Dow, " " tax collector	200 00
	31	Mary J. Blake, " " auditor	5 00
	31	John E. Bennett, " " "	5 00
	31	Myron Haley, " " supervisor	24 00
		Total	$774 00

Town Officers' Expenses

Mar.	23	Automotive Service Bureau	$3 05
	23	E. R. Dale, printing town reports	175 50
	28	Selectmen attending tax commission meeting	14 50
	30	Dow Manufacturing Co., dog tags	5 08
Apr.	18	Otis A. Hersey, stamps, paper, telephoning	10 45

Apr. 18	Edson C. Eastman Co., supplies	$4 19
18	Automotive Service Bureau, clerk's supplies	3 83
19	Selectmen, reappraising property and attending Concord meeting	20 50
24	Ossipee Insurance Agency, collector's bond	15 00
24	Hattie Hersey, board of town officers	10 00
May 10	A. E. Kenison, Reemployment Office	32 00
28	Edson C. Eastman Co., dog license blanks	2 10
28	Automotive Service Bureau, clerk supplies	2 55
June 16	Granite State News, dog notices	2 00
16	Automotive Service Bureau, clerk supplies	3 11
Aug. 13	" " " " "	8 25
Sept. 8	" " "	2 27
Nov. 1	J. P. Melzer, 100 dog license notices	75
17	Myron Roberts, 50 check lists	17 25
Dec. 27	Forrest Hodgdon, helping surveyor on Lake Road, 3 days at trial, preambulating Wolfeboro and Tuftonboro town line	14 00
1935		
Jan. 8	Automotive Service Bureau, clerk supplies	2 13
29	W. J. Britton, town treasurer's bond	25 00
29	Frank S. Bennett, 3 days at Lake Road hearing	9 00
29	Edwin B. Edgerly, 3 days at Lake Road hearing	9 00
31	Selectmen, telephone bill	12 80
31	A. N. Dow, postage, printing, paper etc.	29 71
31	Granite State News, printing ads	2 75
31	Delma McIntire, trips to Plymouth, Portland and telephoning	21 50

Jan. 31 Selectmen, trips to Concord, Relief
business and Island business etc. $34 50
31 Granite State News, selectmen's notices   3 25
31 Hattie Hersey, board of town officers   6 50
31 Marion Horner, town clerk's bond   5 00
31   "   "   copying inventory
and supplies   18 50
31 Otis A. Hersey, motor boat hire, taking
Tax Commissioner to Samoset Island   1 00

Total $527 02

Town Hall Expenses

Apr. 5 Wolfeboro Press, 300 ballots $3 75
June 15 Harry L. Davis, painting town hall in part   50 00
July 6   "   "   "   "   "   "   " full   46 00
Dec. 8 John F. Piper, services as janitor,
lamp chimney and oil   5 25

Total $105 00

Police Department

1935
Jan. 30 Milton Lord, services at
Melvin dances in part $13 00
30 Charles E. Hersey, services at town hall
and special duty   16 75
30 Henry F. Hayes, special services   6 00
31 Selectmen, care of 16 tramps   18 00

Total $53 75

Fire Department

Apr. 24	C. W. Johnson, express on fire pumps	$1 47
July 6	Wolfeboro Fire Precinct, Whittle camp fire	90 00
6	" " " McKean fire	53 50
6	E. B. Edgerly, watchers at two fires	20 50
6	N. H. Forestry Dept., 6 pumps	22 50
Oct. 2	E. B. Edgerly, forest fires	31 95
1935		
Jan. 31	E. B. Edgerly, attendance at fires	
	and postage on 58 permits	8 74
	Total	$228 66

Insurance

July 6	J. C. Avery, insurance on Town Hall	$62 60
1935		
Jan. 31	J. C. Avery, insurance on library books	3 00
31	" " " Workman's Compensation	264 63
	Total	$330 23

Bounties

Jan. 31	Selectmen, 120 hedgehog noses	$24 00
	Total	$24 00

LIST OF PEOPLE KILLING HEDGEHOGS 1924

Name	Number	Amount
Bernard Haley	11	$2 20
Kenneth "	7	1 40
Chas. Allen	3	60
Frank "	1	20
Geo. Cheney	1	20
James Bennett	4	80
Douglas "	2	40
John E. Bennett	4	80
John Hersey	3	60
Edwin "	1	20
Forrest Boardman	2	40
Ralph Bean	1	20
Vincent Bunce	1	20
E. B. Edgerly	5	1 00
Fred Colby	10	2 00
Harvey Ladd, Jr.	1	20
David Adams	1	20
Walter Senior	1	20
Forrest Hodgdon	13	2 60
Harold Bisbee	1	20
Wesley Woodmancy	5	1 00
Ernest Riley	17	3 40
Frank Reed	3	60
Clifton Smith	4	80
Roland Dow	1	20
Junior "	3	60
Edward Roghaar	2	40
Geo. Roberts	2	40
Chas. Hoyt	1	20
Harold Sargent	1	20
Henry Hayes	6	1 20
Roy Rudolph	2	40
	120	$24 00

Chapman School House

May 18 Tuftonboro School District, school building $1 00

Health

Jan. 31 Huggins Hospital, appropriation $100 00

Vital Statistics

Jan. 31 Marion L. Horner, recording marriages,
births and deaths $4 75

Highways and Bridges

Town Maintenance

Mar. 19 Delma McIntire, Road Agent,			snow removal	$300 00
23 Delma McIntire,			snow removal	615 09
Apr. 7 "	"		summer work	76 84
24 "	"	"	"	281 77
May 5 "	"			300 25
14 "				229 87
21 "	"			94 03
June 9 "				144 19
16 "	"	"	"	143 16
23 "				142 25
30		"	"	121 33
July 14 "	"		Melvin Wharf work	96 00
Aug. 4 "	"		summer work	37 58

Aug. 27	Delma McIntire, summer work	$55 65
Nov. 10	" " " "	87 25
Dec. 27	" " plank, gas, labor etc.	19 25
1935		
Jan. 7	" " winter work	245 19
31	" " " "	411 47
	Total	$3 401 17

Bushes

Aug. 18	Delma McIntire	$68 33
27	" "	155 17
Sept. 3	"	77 50
22		54 50
Nov. 10	"	36 33
Dec. 27	" "	8 00
	Total	$399 83

General Expenses of Highway Department

1934

Mar. 6	C. Wesley Johnson, express on tractor parts	$4 47
16	" " " " " " "	23 59
23	Meredith Elec. Light Co., tractor house lights	1 50
23	Clark Wilcox Co., grousers etc.	161 87
28	P. I. Perkins, tractor parts	110 41
31	H. F. Hayes, labor on tractor	18 00
Apr. 18	Berger Metal Culvert Co., culverts	46 62
18	Frank S. Bennett, labor and supplies on tractor house	10 57

Apr.	24	Delma McIntire, labor on tractor	$78 61
	24	Chester Thomas, stove for tractor house	3 00
May	1	John Piper, work on snow fence	3 00
	1	Carl ″ ″ ″ ″ ″	3 00
	5	Delma McIntire, ″ ″ ″ ″	15 99
	10	Meredith Elec. Light Co., tractor house lights	3 66
	28	Delma McIntire, work on snow fence	31 65
June	16	Roscoe Adjutant, carting snow fence	5 33
July	6	Meredith Elec. Light Co., tractor house lights	3 00
	14	Delma McIntire, material for Melvin Wharf	76 66
Aug.	4	″ ″ Banfield road	28 50
	13	Meredith Elec. Light Co., tractor house lights	1 50
	27	Delma McIntire, Tombs road	16 70
	30	John Piper, work on Ledge Hill dump	6 67
Sept.	8	Meredith Elec. Light Co., tractor house lights	1 50
	26	Berger Metal Culvert Co., Federal Con.	36 11
Oct.	6	Delma McIntire, pick handles, freight acc.	14 10
	27	N. H. State Treas., tar and cold patching	15 68
Nov.	1	Meredith Elec. Light Co., tractor house lights	3 00
	10	Delma McIntire, Hesslor road	37 07
	17	Wolfeboro Lumber Co., tractor windshield	8 70
	24	Delma McIntire, snow fence	78 00
Dec.	5	Berger Metal Culvert Co., culverts	36 71
	5	Meredith Elec. Light Co., tractor house lights	1 50
	5	Forrest Hodgdon, 3 trips to Concord	
		for tractor parts and labor on tractor	46 90
	8	Wolfeboro Garage, refacing tractor valves	1 25
	8	″ Falls Garage, labor on	
		tractor cylinder head	1 50
	14	P. I. Perkins Co., grouvers, grease,	
		and tractor parts	148 04
	14	Harold Bisbee, labor on tractor etc.	8 33
	27	Delma McIntire, Hesslor road	9 00
	27	″ ″ alcohol, repairs on tractor	
		and fitting V plow	48 16

Dec. 27 Forrest Hodgdon, labor on tractor and
V plow, wood, freight and paid for
electric welding $38 67

1935
Jan. 4 L. O. Moulton, dynamite etc.   2 73
    5 Meredith Elec. Light Co., tractor house lights   1 50
  25 Henry F. Hayes, labor on tractor   42 38
  31 Delma McIntire,   ″   ″   ″   102 10
  31 Maine Steel Products Co., tractor parts   43 71
  31 Meredith Elec. Light Co., tractor house lights   1 50

Total $1 382 44

New Equipment

Dec. 17 P. I. Perkins Co., 2 V L 76 snow plows $710 60

Libraries

1935
Jan. 17 G. S. Horner, library fund $81 50

Town Poor

Dec. 5 N. H. Relief Administration, town's share $113 51
1935
Jan. 8 G. S. Horner, supplies for Charles Hoyt $8 86
   8 N. H. Relief Administration, town's share   51 01
  31 C. W. Pinkham & Co., supplies
for Forrest Hersey's family   20 44
  31 G. S. Horner, supplies for Charles Hoyt   10 00
  31 N. H. Relief Administration, bal. town's share   50

Total $204 32

Patriotic Purposes

Jan. 31 Harry Harriman Post $25 00

Interest

July 18	Wolfeboro Nat'l. Bank, short term note		$25 00
27	" " " long " "		100 00
Sept. 26	" " " " " "		50 00
Dec. 27	W. W. Thomas, guardian for		
		Hattie McIntire	88 33
1935			
Jan. 31	Wolfeboro Nat'l. Bank, int. on		
		long term note	50 00
31	Wolfeboro Nat'l. Bank, int. on		
		long term note	50 00
	Total		$363 33

Discounts and Abatements

Jan. 31	A. N. Dow, abatements	$135 40
31	" " " discounts	163 27
31	Marion L. Horner, auto permits	61 50
31	A. N. Dow, balance on abatements	2 00
	Total	$362 17

List of Abatements

PROPERTY

Mary P. Hersey, heirs, fire	$4 00
John E. Kurth, soldier's exemption	20 00
Jesse Sargent, public water	3 00
Geo. E. Wiggin, " "	3 00
John G. Snow, out of town	3 40
Harley A. Flint, overtax	12 00
Paul Loomis, Est., "	10 00
Samuel Shaw, "	20 00
E. M. Sams	20 00
	$95 40

Polls

Frank Bean,	out of town	$2 00
Mary "	" " "	2 00
Alva Cain,		2 00
Beatrice Carpenter,	" " "	2 00
Louis "		2 00
Emily McKean,		2 00
Hazel Morris,		2 00
Sidney Patchett,	" " "	2 00
Mary O. "	" " "	2 00
Elsie Snow,		2 00
Hutson "		2 00
Lawrence West,	" " "	2 00
Irene West,		2 00
O. V. Bennett, over 70		2 00
Fred Leavitt, " 70		2 00
E. R. Whitten. " 70		2 00
N. J. Wilcox, " 70		2 00
Thomas Hopkinson, unable to pay		2 00
Sarah " " " "		2 00
John E. Kurth, soldier		2 00
Arthur Smith, paid in Ossipee		2 00
		$42 00
	Total	$137 40

Legal Advice

July   6 Cooper and Hall, information
.................about Chapman Schoolhouse $4 00
Dec.   4 Walter S. Wheeler, City Engineer
.................of Dover, Services on Lake Road 112 50
1935
Jan. 23 Walter S. Wheeler, Services in
.................Lake Road case in full 31 25
.................................Total $147 75

New Construction

Tuftonboro Neck and Wawbeek Roads

June 8 E. B. Edgerly, sanding $149 40
.........19 E. B. Edgerly, oiling 49 00
July   6 N. H. State Treasurer, oil 447 20
Aug. 18 Delma McIntire, patching 104 50
.........27 N. H. State Treasurer,
.................................cold patch material 117 00
Sept. 22 Delma McIntire, filling holes 97 95
.................................Total $965 05

State Aid Construction

Sept. 13 N. H. State Treasurer,
.................30% State Aid Construction $524 08
Dec. 20 N. H. State Treasurer, balance town
.................share State Aid Construction 1 220 82
.................................Total $1 744 90

Emergency Relief Unemployment

Sept. 22	Delma McIntire		$433 98
Oct. 6	"	"	537 20
13	"	"	480 40
18			390 15
27			361 30
Dec. 5	"		37 67
		Total	$2 240 70

Indebtedness

TEMPORARY LOANS

July 18	Wolfeboro Nat'l. Bank	$2 000 00
1935		
Jan. 31	Wolfeboro Nat'l. Bank, note	2 000 00
	Total	$4 000 00

Payments to Other Governmental Divisions

July 18	Eugene I. Smith, ½ County tax	$2 316 75
Nov. 1	" " " balance County tax	2 316 75
	Total	$4 633 50
Dec. 8	Chas. T. Patten, State tax	$2 379 00

Schools

Oct. 24	T. W. Cellarius, Treasurer	$1 000 00
Nov. 27	" " " "	1 000 00
Dec. 17	" " "	1 000 00
1935		
Jan. 31	T. W. Cellarius, bal. school appropriation	4 040 35
31	" " " 1933 dog licenses	188 40
	Total	$7 228 75

Tuftonboro Neck and Wawbeek Roads

SANDING AND OILING, JUNE 4 - 5 - 6 AND 18, 1934

EDWIN B. EDGERLY, Foreman.

Name	Kind of Work	No. of Days	Rate	Amt. Paid
Walter Skinner,	shoveling	3	$3 00	$9 00
Thomas Hopkinson,	"	2	3 00	6 00
Clarence Staples,	"	3	3 00	9 00
H. Woodmancy,		3	3 00	9 00
William Chick,	..	2	3 00	6 00
W. Hopkinson,		3	3 00	9 00
John I. Edgerly,		1	3 00	3 00
E. B. Edgerly,		3½	3 00	10 50
Arthur Keenan,	trucking	4¼	8 00	34 00
Joseph Whitten,	"	3	8 00	24 00
Avert Pineo,	"	2	8 00	16 00
Leon Dore,	"	2	8 00	16 00
John E. Bennett,	spreading	1	3 00	3 00
John Bennett,	"	1	3 00	3 00
John Hardie,	"	1	3 00	3 00
Curtis Edgerly,		1	3 00	3 00
W. Hopkinson,		1	3 00	3 00
Filburt Ridlon,		1	3 00	3 00
Will Chick,	"	1	3 00	3 00
Charles Haley,	"	1	3 00	3 00
Burton Whitten,		1	3 00	3 00
David Bennett,		½	3 00	1 50
Wm. Skinner,		½	3 00	1 50
Russell Whitten,		1	2 00	2 00
Hazen Whittier,	"	1	2 00	2 00
129 Loads of sand		@ 10¢		12 90

	Total	$198 40
N. H. State Treasurer, oil		447 20
N. H. State Treasurer, cold patching material		117 00
Delma McIntire, patching		104 50
Delma McIntire, filling holes		97 95
	Total	$965 05

Report of Road Agent

DELMA McINTIRE

For week ending Mar. 17, 1934

Delma McIntire, tractor and truck plow	$112 75
Graydon Morris, helper	66 25
Ernest Dow, tractor	8 25
Gilmore Morris, helper	17 50
Carroll Lamprey, "	13 00
Frank Bennett, "	14 50
" " shoveling snow	6 00
Ralph Piper, " "	11 00
Robert Straw,	4 00
Levi Ayers,	4 00
Carl Piper,	14 50
George Stillings, "	16 17
Roscoe "	15 17
Preston Piper,	15 50
Hutson Snow,	15 50
John Piper,	15 50
Forrest Hersey,	16 17
Steve Tupeck,	11 17
James Bennett,	16 17

Jack Hlushuk,	shoveling snow	$10 50
Edwin Hersey,	" "	12 50
Harry A. Davis,		10 33
Leon Dore,	" "	7 67
Curtis Edgerly,		6 17
Benjamin Ferguson,	"	7 00
Carl B. Johnson, gas		25 29
Delbert Haley,	shoveling snow	1 67
Thomas Hopkinson,	" "	3 67
Arthur Keenan,		3 00
William Chick,	" "	6 00
G. S. Horner, gas and alcohol		22 63
Henry E. Woodmancy, shoveling snow		9 00
C. Wesley	" " "	9 00
Wilfred Hopkinson,	"	3 00
Forrest Hodgdon, tractor and gas		137 40
Harold Bisbee, helper		46 25
Wilbur Abbott, shoveling snow		18 67
Frank Evans,	" "	16 00
Roy Manly,		9 00
Wendal Emery,	" "	8 67
Roy Ham,		18 00
Albert Dow,		6 17
George Roberts,	"	15 00
Edward Shannon,	"	13 67
Herbert Ayers,	"	4 00
Oliver Allen,	"	2 00
Forrest Boardman,	"	1 33
Gerald McDuffee,	"	2 00
Irving	"	2 00
Roy Rudolph,		2 00
Edward Roghaar,	" "	2 00

E. B. Edgerly, shoveling snow	$3 00
C. W. Pinkham Co., gas	44 84
Ernest Hunter, shoveling snow	2 33
Bradbury Hunter, " "	2 33
Arthur Davis,	3 00
Kenneth Haley,	2 50
Edward Allen, "	2 50
Charles "	2 50
" Haley,	2 50
Earl Cheney,	2 50
Albert "	2 50
Wyatt "	2 50
Weston Stevens, "	2 50
Howard Haley,	2 50
Bernard "	2 50
Total	$915 09

For week ending Apr. 7, 1934

Delma McIntire, trucking gravel	$35 50
Arthur Keenan, " "	18 00
Ralph Piper, shoveling gravel	7 67
Graydon Morris, " "	2 50
Douglas Bennett, "	6 00
Harry Hooper,	1 67
Gilmore Morris,	1 50
Delbert Haley,	1 50
Gordon Cheney, "	2 50
Total	$76 84

For week ending Apr. 14, 1934

Delma McIntire, trucking gravel	$47 00
Joseph Whitten, " "	27 00
Leon Dore, ". "	24 00
Ralph Piper, shoveling "	9 00
John " "	9 00

Carl Piper, shoveling gravel	$9 00
George Stillings, ″ ″	9 00
Frank Bennett, ″ ″	13 50
Graydon Morris, leveling	9 00
Woodbury Willand, gravel	15 60
Douglas Bennett, helper	67
Total	$172 77

For week ending Apr. 21, 1934

Delma McIntire, trucking gravel	$27 00
Graydon Morris, helper	9 00
Frank Bennett, shoveling	4 50
Edwin Hersey, ″	7 50
John Piper,	4 50
Carl ″	.4 50
George Stillings, ″	1 50
Forrest Hersey, ″	3 00
Will Bean,	3 00
Maurice Mack, ″	3 00
Leon Dore, truck	13 50
Joseph Whitten, ″	9 00
Roscoe Adjutant, team scraping	6 00
William Burrows, ″ ″	.4 00
Edward Shannon, work on road	3 00
Herbert Ayers, ″ ″ ″	3 00
James Bennett, helping on scraper	3 00
Total	$109 00

For week ending Apr. 28, 1934

Delma McIntire, trucking gravel	$27 00
Joseph Whitten, ″ ″	9 00
Leon Dore, ″	9 00
Graydon Morris, leveling	6 00
Forrest Hersey, shoveling .	3 00

Maurice Mack, shoveling	$3 00
Edwin Hersey, "	3 00
John Piper,	3 00
Carl "	3 00
Will Bean, leveling "	3 00
Roscoe Adjutant, team scraping	24 00
Arthur Keenan, trucking	18 00
Benjamin Ferguson, helper	6 00
Woodbury Willand, gravel	13 30
Herman Hodgdon, helper	3 00
Harry Hooper, work on culverts	3 00
Total	$136 30

For week ending May 5, 1934

Delma McIntire, trucking gravel and scraping	$25 00
Roger Davis, " "	18 00
Howard Colby,	18 00
Ernest Hunter, "	18 00
Harry L. Davis, shoveling	6 00
Milton Lord, " and gravel	21 45
Russell Watson,	6 00
John Bean,	6 00
Theodore Cellarius, "	6 00
Weston Stevens,	6 00
Charles Crook,	6 00
Chester Thomas,	2 00
Wesley Woodmancy, "	3 00
Gilmore Morris, leveling	6 00
Horace Walker, "	4 50
Edward Shannon, team scraping	12 00
Total	$163 95

For week ending May 12, 1934

Delma McIntire, trucking gravel	$30 00

Ausbrey Dow,	trucking gravel	$27 00
Maurice Welch,	" "	27 00
Roy Ham,	"	27 00
Wilbur Abbott,	leveling	9 00
Wendal Emery,	shoveling	9 00
Herbert Ayers,	"	9 00
Edwin Stillings,		9 00
Clifton Smith,	"	6 00
Harold Bisbee,	"	9 00
Frank Evans,	"	9 00
Eli Davis,		8 50
Frank Reed,	"	8 17
Jesse Sargent,	141 loads gravel	14 10
Charles A. Thompson,	64 loads gravel	6 40
Joseph Whitten,	trucking gravel	4 50
George Stillings,	helper	1 50
Ernest Hunter,	35 loads gravel	3 50
E. B. Edgerly,	87 " "	8 70
John A. Edgerly,	25 " "	2 50
Carl Johnson,	shoveling	1 00
	Total	$229 87

For week ending May 19, 1934

Delma McIntire,	trucking gravel	$36 00
Ernest Hunter,	" "	9 00
James Bennett,	shoveling	7 50
Edwin Hersey,	"	2 33
Herbert Ayers,		6 00
Edward Roghaar,	"	6 00
Gerald McDuffee,	"	6 00
Irving	"	3 00

Wendal Emery, shoveling	$2 50
Joe LeBlanc, gravel 58 loads @ 15¢	8 70
George Stillings, work on road	3 00
Philip Hunt, " " "	4 00
Total	$94 03

For week ending June 2, 1934

Delma McIntire, trucking gravel	$11 00
Maurice Mack, helper	3 00
Total	$14 00

For week ending June 9, 1934

Delma McIntire, trucking gravel	$42 50
Maurice Mack, shoveling	15 00
Wesley Woodmancy, "	13 50
Joseph Whitten, truck	11 00
Peter Cordeau, work on road	8 70
Ernest Hunter, truck	9 00
Irving McDuffee, stringers and labor for bridge	5 00
Gerald " labor on bridge	5 00
Joseph LeBlanc, gravel	2 10
Roy Rudolph, shoveling	4 00
Ausbrey Dow, lumber	13 39
Edward N. Roghaar, labor	1 00
Total	$130 19

For week ending June 16, 1934

Delma McIntire, scraping roads	$31 50
Maurice Mack, helper	15 00
Wesley Woodmancy, "	15 00
William Burrows, team	30 00
Ernest Hunter, machine	20 00
Roscoe Adjutant, team	30 00
Bernard Haley, work	83
Howard Haley, "	83
Total	$143 16

For week ending June 23, 1934

Delma McIntire, scraping roads	$22 50
Maurice Mack, helper	12 00
Wesley Woodmancy, "	15 00
Will Burrows, team	30 00
Roscoe Adjutant, "	6 00
Thomas Blaisdell, "	24 00
C. L. Jenness, bridge plank	6 75
Frank Forsythe, helper	3 00
Ernest Hunter, machine	20 00
James Bennett, helper	3 00
Total	$142 25

For week ending June 30, 1934

Delma McIntire, scraping roads	$45 00
Maurice Mack, helper	15 00
Wesley Woodmancy, "	15 00
Ernest Hunter, machine	20 00
William Burrows, team	6 00
Thomas Blaisdell, "	6 00
Fred Fisher, helper	9 00
Fred Colbath, "	3 00
Daniel Palmer, picking rocks	2 33
Total	$121 33

For week ending July 14, 1934

Delma McIntire, trucking lumber etc.	$31 50
Maurice Mack, helper	19 50
Wesley Woodmancy, "	19 50
Howard Colby, trucking	18 00
Bradbury Hunter, team	3 00
Forrest Hersey	1 50
James Bennett	1 50
Roscoe Stillings	1 50
Total	$96 00

For week ending July 21, 1934

Delma McIntire, scraping, work on bridge	$23 25
Maurice Mack, helper	7 00
Ernest Hunter, machine	2 00
Wesley Woodmancy, helper	5 33
Total	$37 58

For week ending Aug. 25, 1934

Delma McIntire, trucking gravel	$33 00
Maurice Mack, helper	11 00
Wesley Woodmancy, "	4 00
Ralph Bean, "	1 00
W. P. Willand, 14 loads gravel	1 40
James Bennett, helper	3 00
Mrs. Anna Richardson, 15 loads gravel	2 25
Total	$55 65

For week ending Nov. 3, 1934

Delma McIntire, gravel	$15 00
Maurice Mack, helper	1 50
Mrs. Anna Richardson, gravel	1 20
Charles Brown, team	6 00
Harold Bisbee, work on road	2 33
Roy Ham, " " "	1 00
Philip Hunt,	9 00
Daniel Palmer, " " "	1 67
Total	$37 70

For week ending Nov. 10, 1934

Delma McIntire, ditches	$15 75
Philip Hunt, "	13 50
Roscoe Adjutant, truck	11 30
Walter Robinson, helper	3 00
Wesley Woodmancy, ditches	3 00
John I. Edgerly, "	3 00
Total	$49 55

For week ending Dec. 1, 1934

Delma McIntire, fixing bridge	$4 50
Maurice Mack, helper	1 50
Ernest Piper, gas	3 40
Fred Foss, sharpening picks	3 40
C. Jenness, plank	6 45
Total	$19 25

For week ending Dec. 29, 1934

Delma McIntire, tractor, truck plow	$33 00
Graydon Morris, helper	10 60
Harold Bisbee, "	24 20
Forrest Hodgdon, tractor and gas	76 38
Total	$144 18

For week ending Jan. 5, 1935

Delma McIntire, tractor, truck plow	$45 00
Graydon Morris, " helper	18 05
Frank Bennett, " "	14 30
Maurice Mack, helper	8 30
James Bennett, "	8 50
Robert Paige,	1 20
Benjamin Ferguson, shoveling	1 33
Curtis Edgerly, "	1 33
Thomas Hopkinson,	1 00
Wilfred "	1 00
Levi Ayers,	1 00
Total	$101 01

For week ending Jan. 12, 1935

Delma McIntire, truck plow, tractor	$44 25
James Bennett, helper	2 80
Maurice Mack, "	7 20
Carl Johnson, gas	6 05
Kenneth Cellarius, helper	7 20
Total	$67 50

For week ending Jan. 31, 1935

Delma McIntire, tractor	$1 50
Edwin Hersey, shoveling	1 67
Jack Hlushuk, "	1 67
Carroll Lamprey, "	1 33
James Bennett,	1 33
George Stillings, "	1 33
John Ayers,	1 33
Forrest Hersey, "	1 33
Carl Piper,	1 33
Preston Piper, "	1 33
Leon Dore, shoveling snow	1 00
Ben Ferguson, " "	2 00
Robert Straw, " "	2 00
Harold Stead,	2 00
Arnold Ridlon,	2 00
Clarence Strout,	2 00
John I. Edgerly,	2 00
Curtis Edgerly,	2 00
Thomas Hopkinson, "	2 17
Wilfred "	2 33
Levi Ayers, " "	2 33
Forrest Hodgdon, tractor and gas	111 25
Jane Welch, gas	6 44
Howard Emery, "	5 00
Harold Bisbee, work on plow	41 60
G. S. Horner, gas and alcohol	16 85
C. W. Pinkham Co., gas and bolts	24 23
Ernest Piper, gas	5 42
Carl Johnson, "	11 62
John Hardie, "	4 88
Delma McIntire, tractor	60 00
Kenneth Cellarius, helper	15 70
Maurice Mack, "	5 00
Total	$343 97
Town Maintenance Total	$3 401 17

Town Maintenance Bushes

For week ending Aug. 18, 1934

John Leary,	cutting bushes	$8 33
Albert Cheney,	" "	18 00
Kenneth Haley,	"	3 00
Edward Allen,	"	12 00
Ralph Bean,		8 00
Will "		8 00
Harry L. Davis,	"	2 00
Foster Davis,		6 00
Russell Watson,	"	3 00
	Total	$68 33

For week ending Aug. 25, 1934

Ralph Bean,	cutting bushes	$14 00
Will "	" "	14 00
Albert Cheney,	"	14 00
George Stillings,		14 00
Maurice Mack,		3 00
Wesley Woodmancy,	"	6 00
James Bennett,		14 00
Harry L. Davis,		3 67
Forrest Boardman,	"	12 00
George Roberts,		12 00
Herbert Ayers,		6 00
Kenneth Haley,	" "	3 00

Russell Watson,	cutting bushes	$4 50
Maurice Bennett,	" "	6 00
John "		6 00
Herman Hodgdon,		6 00
Albert Cheney,		17 00
	Total	$155 17

For week ending Sept. 1, 1934

Ralph Bean,	cutting bushes	$12 00
Will "	" "	12 00
George Stillings,	"	12 00
James Bennett,		12 00
George Roberts,	"	10 00
Herbert Ayers,		7 50
Albert Cheney,		6 00
Forrest Boardman,	"	6 00
	Total	$77 50

For week ending Sept. 8, 1934

George Stillings,	cutting bushes	$12 00
James Bennett,	" "	12 00
Ralph Bean,		12 00
Will "		12 00
Forrest Boardman,	"	4 50
Charles Hoyt,		2 00
	Total	$54 50

For week ending Oct. 6, 1934

Charles Brown,	cutting bushes	$12 00
Forrest Hersey,	" "	9 00
George Stillings,		3 00
Ralph Bean,		3 00
Will "		3 00
Philip Hunt,		5 00
James Bennett,		1 33
	Total	$36 33

For week ending Nov 24, 1934

Delma McIntire, trucking bushes		$6 00
John I. Edgerly, helper	.	2 00
	Total	$8 00
	Total for bushes	$399 83

General Expense Snowfence

For week ending May 19, 1934

Kenneth Haley,	taking	up	fence		$1 50
Edward Allen,	"	"	"		1 50
Edwin Hersey,	"	"	"		2 00
Frank Bennett,	"	"	"		2 00
John Piper,	"	"	"		2 00
Benjamin Ferguson,	"	"	"		2 33
Arthur Keenan,	"	.	"	"	2 33
Levi Ayers,	"	"	"		2 33
			Total		$15 99

For week ending May 26, 1934

Delma McIntire, trucking fence		$9 00
Maurice Mack,	helper	3 00
Earl Cheney,	"	3 00
Roy Ham,	snowfence	4 00
Harold Bisbee,	"	1 66
George Roberts,	"	2 33
Forrest Hodgdon,	"	8 66
	Total	$31 65

For week ending Nov. 24, 1934

Delma McIntire,	trucking fence			$18 00
George Stillings,	putting	up	fence	6 00
Gilmore Morris,	"	"	"	6 00
Maurice Mack,	"	"	"	6 00

Wesley Woodmancy, putting up fence	$6	00
Horace Walker, " " "	6	00
Forrest Hodgdon, trucking fence	18	00
Carlton Eldridge, putting up fence	6	00
Harold Bisbee, " " "	6	00
Total	$78	00

Banfil Road

For week ending July 28, 1934

Delma McIntire, fixing road	$13	50
Maurice Mack, helper	9	00
Wesley Woodmancy, "	6	00
Total	$28	50

Tomb Road

For week ending Aug. 25, 1934

Delma McIntire, trucking gravel	$9	00
Maurice Mack, helper	3	00
Wesley Woodmancy, "	3	00
John A. Edgerly, gravel	1	70
Total	$16	70

Hesslor Road

For week ending Nov. 10, 1934

Delma McIntire, trucking gravel	$26	00
John I. Edgerly, helper	8	67
Edwin Edgerly, gravel	1	80
W. P. Willand, "		60
Total	$37	07

For week ending Nov. 24, 1934

Delma McIntire, scraping road, gravel	$7 50
John I. Edgerly, helper	1 50
Total	$9 00

General Expense Sanding

Delma McIntire, sanding road	$18 00
Frank Bennett, helper	8 67
Oscar Whedon, sanding	67
Roy Varney, battery service	3 50
Robie's Garage, welding	35 87
George Wakefield, labor on tractor	11 90
Total	$78 61

For week ending July 14, 1934

The Diamond Match Co., lumber	$64 31
G. S. Horner, spikes etc.	11 10
Allen E. Crosby, wharf pins	1 25
Total	$76 66

For week ending Oct. 6, 1934

G. S. Horner, pick handles	$3 00
J. A. Sullivan, " "	45
Peterson Motor Express, culvert	3 00
Austin Western Road Machinery Co.	6 30
Boston & Maine R. R., freight	1 35
Total	$14 10

For week ending Dec. 15, 1934

Delma McIntire, work and repairs	$12 35
George Wakefield, labor " "	26 80
G. S. Horner, wire	91
Carl Johnson, gas for mixer	2 10
Maurice Mack, work on plow	3 00
Graydon Morris, " " "	3 00
Total	$48 16

For week ending Jan. 31, 1935.

Roy Varney, gas etc.	$18 50
Geo. Wakefield, repairs on tractor	34 75
Delma McIntire, work " "	18 85
James Bennett, " " "	10 50
Frank " " " "	4 00
Maurice Mack, " " "	6 50
Elbridge Robie, welding	9 00
Total	$102 10

E. R. U.

Sept. 22	Delma McIntire	$373 83
29	" "	537 20
Oct. 6	"	480 40
13		450 30
20		361 30
Nov. 24	" . "	37 67
	Total	$2 240 70

Tuftonboro Neck and Wawbeek

DELMA McINTIRE, Foreman

Arthur Keenan,	1 day truck	$9 00
Roscoe Adjutant,	1 " "	9 00
Joseph Whitten,	1 " "	9 00
Leon Dore,	1 '	9 00
Delma McIntire,	7 " "	63 00
Russell Watson,	1 " labor	3 00
Chester Thomas,	1 " "	3 00
John I. Edgerly,	1 " "	3 00
Thomas Hopkinson,	1 " "	3 00

Wesley Woodmancy,	7 days labor	$21 00
Henry "	1 day "	3 00
Clarence Staples,	1 " '	3 00
John F. Piper,	1	3 00
Charles Crook,	1	3 00
Wyatt Cheney,	1	3 00
Edward Allen,	1	3 00
Walter Skinner,	1	3 00
Ralph Bean,	1	3 00
Will "	1	3 00
Maurice Mack,	5 days '	15 00
Arthur Bean,	4⅔ " "	14 00
Delma McIntire,	1 day "	4 50
Mrs. A. A. Richardson, 43 loads gravel @ 15¢		6 45
W. P. Willand, 19 loads sand @ 10¢		1 90
Charles Copp, 16 " " @ 10¢		1 60
	Total	$202 45

DATE OF CREATION	TRUST FUNDS PURPOSE OF CREATION	HOW INVESTED	Amount of Principal	Rate of Interest	Bal. of Inco on Hand at ginning of Y	Income During Ye	Expende During Ye	Bal. of Inco on Hand a End of Yea
Nov. 5, 1889	George G. Fox, for Tibbetts, Interest only	Rochester Bank	$ 300 00	3 %	$3 16	$10 96	$5 00	$69 12
May 9, 1918	Chamberlain Fund, for Chamberlain Lot, Tuftonboro Nk Cemetery, Interest only	The Amoskeag Savings Bank, Manchester, N.H.	100 00	3½	17 04	4 07	5 00	16 11
Nov. 20, 1920	Tuftonboro Neck Cemetery Fund, Interest only	Liberty Bond	200 00	4¼				
Sept. 4, 1929	Tuftonboro Nk Cemetery Fund, Interest only	Wolfeboro Bank	125 00	3	26 12	14 52	7 50	33 14
Sept. 9, 1921	Rendall Fund, for D. A. Wiggin Lot, Edgerly Cemetery, Interest only	Wolfeboro Bank	D0 00	3	19 68	4 45	3 50	20 63
July 1, 1929	Susan A. Thompson Whidden, Jones , In e est only	Wolfeboro Bank	500 00	3	75 63	17 38	8 70	84 31
Apr. 21, 30	s and Amos Kimball Fund, Edgerly Cemetery, Interest only	The keag Savings Bank, Manchester, N.H.	100 00	3½	4 65	3 68	2 75	5 58
Mar. 1, 1933	Annabelle Thompson Fund, Thompson Cemetery, In erest only	Wolfeboro Bank	75 00	3	12	2 26	2 25	13

This is to certify that the information contained in this report is compl te and corr et, to the best of our knowledge and belief.

January 31, 1935.

Auditor's Certificate

February 1, 1935

We certify that we have examined the foregoing accounts, and find them correct and properly vouched for.

MARY J. BLAKE ⎫
JOHN E. BENNETT ⎬ Auditors.
⎭

Tuftonboro Free Library Report Year 1934

Received from town	$81 50	
On hand from previous year	1 53	
		$83 03
Paid Mrs. Edwin C. Hersey, librarian	$50 00	
Paid for books	31 40	
Cost of transportation	1 04	$82 44
Balance on hand		$ 59

Mrs. Mitchell gave the Library 2 books, Mr. Eugene Richardson donated 5 books and Caryl Dow also gave 8 books.

We extend to these people our appreciation for their gifts to the Library.

MRS. EDWIN C. HERSEY ⎫ Trustees of
MRS. EDA M. DAVIS ⎬ Tuftonboro
GEORGE S. HORNER ⎭ Free Library

INVENTORY

OF THE

RESIDENT

AND

NON-RESIDENT

TAXPAYERS

OF THE TOWN OF

TUFTONBORO

N. H.

1934

INVENTORY

OF THE RESIDENT TAXPAYERS

OF THE TOWN OF TUFTONBORO

RESIDENT INVOICE AND TAXES FOR THE YEAR 1934		
NAME AND DESCRIPTION	VALUATION	TOTAL TAX
Abbott, Wilbur		
3a John Q. Haley	$600 00	
1 Cow	35	$635 00 $12 70
Adjutant, Eliza		
30a	100	100 2 00
Adjutant, Roscoe		
1a Home place	950	
1a Berry lot	25	
30a Bickford lot	200	
2 Horses	80	
1 Cow	30	
Theo. Hunt camp	200	1 485 29 70
Adjutant, W. W.		
30a Home place	600	
1 Cow	30	630 12 60
Allen, Etta and Oliver		
75a Home place	800	
80a Leavitt lot	300	
1 Horse	50	1 150 23 00
Allen, George W.		
2a Home place	300	
3 Cows	70	
10a Hall field	200	570 11 40
Ames, Maynard J.		
Over exemption		
10a Frances Bennett	500	500 10 00

RESIDENT INVOICE AND TAXES FOR THE YEAR 1934

NAME AND DESCRIPTION	VALUATION		TOTAL TAX
Ayers, Herbert			
75a Home place	$800 00		
1 Horse	50		
1 Cow	20	$870 00	$17 40
Ayers, James, heirs			
60ι	700	700	14 00
Ayers, John			
55a Pasture.	200		
90a Home place	800		
½a M. L. McDuffee	1 200		
4ι Levi Ferguson	2 000	4 200	84 00
Banfield, Stanley M.			
1a Camp and lot	1 000	1 000	20 00
Baxter, George			
2 Cows	75		
1 Neat stock	25	100	2 00
Bean, Arthur M.			
32a Echo Farm	2 500		
195ι G. T. Dudley	1 200		
1 Horse	75		
2 Cows	75	3 850	77 00
Bean, Cora, Est.			
70a	1 200	1 200	24 00
Bean, John W.			
10a Wood lot	50		
46a Streeter lot	200		
50a Kenison lot	400	650	13 00
Bean, Mark O., Est.			
Horner lot	50	50	1 00
Bean, Mary F.			
8a	500	500	10 00
Bean, Ralph L.			
85a Home place	1 920		
1 Horse	50		
4 Cows	90	2 060	41 20

RESIDENT INVOICE AND TAXES FOR THE YEAR 1934		
NAME AND DESCRIPTION	VALUATION	TOTAL TAX
Bean, Ula L.		
20a Peavey lot	$200 00	$200 00	$4 00
Bean, Willie L.		
15ı	150	
1 Cow	20	170	3 40
Bennett, C. H.		
15ı Davis lot	100	100	2 00
Bennett, Frank S.		
2ı Home place	500	500	10 00
Bennett, John E.		
113ı Farm	7 300	
95ı Haley pasture	300	
1 Horse	40	
6 Cows	200	
4 Neat stock	100	7 940	158 80
Bennett, Maurice		
100ı Farm	1 700	
4 Cows	100	1 800	36 00
Bennett, Orsino V.		
95ı Farm	2 050	
50ı ½ Gilman lot	200	
2 Horses	90	
4 Cow	100	2 440	48 80
Bennett, Ralph V.		
50a ½ Gilman lot	200	
8a Meadow	100	
460 Fowl	295	645	12 90
Bisbee, Addie		
40a Pasture	150	150	3 00
Bisbee, Archer C.		
1a Home place	200	200	4 00
Bisbee, Arthur H.		
½a Minnie White	300	
1½a E. E. Ingalls	50	
Pine lot	100	
1 Cow	35	485	9 70

RESIDENT INVOICE AND TAXES FOR THE YEAR 1934

NAME AND DESCRIPTION	VALUATION		TOTAL TAX
Bisbee, Wilbur			
1a Home place	$500 00	$500 00	$10 00
Blaisdell, Thomas H.			
120a Farm	1 100		
15a Meadow	50		
40a Thos. French	1 400		
8 Cows	280		
2 Mules	100		
2 Neat stock	30		
83 Fowl	12 25	2 972 25	59 45
Blake, Joseph C.			
3a George Morrison	2 200		
12a C. D. Horne	50		
1 Cow	25	2 275	45 50
Blount, Irene G.			
1a Camp and lot	3 000		
1 Boat	300	3 300	66 00
Boyden, Harriett			
2a Home place	1 500	1 500	30 00
Bray, Thomas			
3a Home place	2 500	2 500	50 00
Brown, Charles H.			
220a Farm	1 700		
2 Horses	200		
5 Cows	150		
1 Neat stock	25		
200 Fowl	100	2 175	43 50
Brown, Harold			
Camp lot	100	100	2 00
Burleigh, Jane			
4a Home place	1 200	1 200	24 00
Burrows, Will			
1 Horse	40	40	80

RESIDENT INVOICE AND TAXES FOR THE YEAR 1934

NAME AND DESCRIPTION	VALUATION		TOTAL TAX
Bushnell, George			
2½a Rollin Jones Jr.	$32 000 00		
4 Boats	4 700	$36 700 00	$734 00
Caverly, Mary			
2a Home place	1 200	1 200	24 00
Caverly, Walter H.			
28a Meadow	100	100	2 00
Cellarius, Edna			
1a Mark Piper	1 200		
18a ⅓ Hersey farm	950		
3a ⅓ Meadow	50	2 200	44 00
Cheney, George M.			
50a Farm	2 200		
1 Horse	35		
3 Cows	100		
1 Neat stock	20	2 355	47 10
Cheney, Gordon			
1 Cow	50	50	1 00
Cheney, Wyatt D.			
25a Freeman Gove	250		
3 Horses	500		
1 Cow	40	790	15 80
Chick, William M.			
40a C. O. Dore	1 500		
1 Neat stock	20		
3 Cows	110	1 630	32 60
Colby, Fred W.			
100a Dame place	400	400	8 00
Copp, Charles F.			
55a Farm	3 500		
2 Cows	85		
500 Fowl	325	3 910	78 20
Cordeau, Peter			
75a Gilman place	900	900	18 00

RESIDENT INVOICE AND TAXES FOR THE YEAR 1934

NAME AND DESCRIPTION	VALUATION		TOTAL TAX
Craig, Edith M.			
85a A. L. Brewster	$3 400 00		
Horner mill site	50		
15½ Haley place	800		
3a Mary Bean	50		
36½ Haley point	6 000		
2a Leon Sheperd	200	$10 500 00	$210 00
Crook, Charles			
O. Richardson	500		
¼a J. A. Stackpole	800	1 300	26 00
Davis, Charles W.			
3a Home place	2 800	2 800	56 00
Davis, Harry A.			
46a Home place	1 000		
1 Horse	30		
1 Cow	25	1 055	21 10
Davis, Harry L.			
6a Home place	500		
2 Cows	45	545	10 90
Dearborn, Estella E.			
Home place	500	500	10 00
Doe, James A., Est.			
76a Farm	1 100	1 100	22 00
Dore, Leon			
1a Drew lot	250		
1 Cow	35		
150 Fowl	72 50	357 50	7 15
Dow, Alvah E.			
72a Farm	2 040		
60a Pasture	250	2 290	45 80
Dow, Ausbrey N.			
2 Horses	140	140	2 80
Dow, Bessie			
Home place	700	700	14 00
Dow, Ernest H.			
3 Cows	100	100	2 00

RESIDENT INVOICE AND TAXES FOR THE YEAR 1934

NAME AND DESCRIPTION	VALUATION		TOTAL TAX
Dreier, Thomas			
400a Asa Thompson	$5 500 00		
Mark Piper	100	$5 600 00	$112 00
Eaton, Charles M.			
142a Farm	5 000	5 000	100 00
Edgerly, Edwin B.			
128a Farm	5 000		
1a Broadview	2 300		
20a Frank Piper	1 000		
2 Cows	80		
3 Neat stock	80		
15 Fowl	12		
2 Oxen	100	8 572	172 44
Edgerly, John A.			
1a Home place	2 500		
23a Piper pasture	500		
Camp	1 500		
25a Frank Piper	200		
50a J. H. Young	650		
120a Lamprey Hill	1 000		
14a Meadow	50		
35a D. D. Wingate	250		
50a Abel Haley	100		
2 Horses	100		
1 Cow	45	6 895	137 90
Edwards, John T.			
1 Horse	40		
1 Cow	30	70	1 40
Edwards, Mary			
25a L. C. Canney	500	500	10 00
Emery, Wendal			
160a Lucy Libby	2 300		
1 Horse	40		
2 Cows	40	2 380	47 60
Evans, Evelyn			
2a Home place	500	500	10 00

RESIDENT INVOICE AND TAXES FOR THE YEAR 1934

NAME AND DESCRIPTION	VALUATION		TOTAL TAX
Fernald, Emma J.			
½a Fernald House	$3 000 00	$3 000 00	$60 00
Fernald, Walter E.			
9a Camp Wawbeek	8 000		
Hoagland Camp	4 500		
Boats	250	12 750	255 00
Ford, John, Est.			
30a Bickford lot	100	100	2 00
Forsythe, Frank S.			
50a Robert McKean	600		
1 Cow	25	625	12 50
Gendro, Clement			
7a Home place	1 200	1 200	24 00
Gilman, Aaron			
6a Home place	500	500	10 00
Gilman, Chester H.			
3 Cows	120	120	2 40
Gilman, Edith B.			
60a Home place	1 500	1 500	30 00
Gordon, Estella D.			
½a Gordon Cottage	1 200		
2a Field	250	1 450	29 00
Haley, Bertha M.			
10a Mountainview Lodge	3 500	3 500	70 00
Haley, Charles E.			
40a Home place	800		
2 Cows	35		
Mill	200	1 035	20 70
Haley, Delbert C.			
2a Home place	200	200	4 00
Ham, Addie E.			
72a Home place	2 200		
10a Pine lot	80		
4a Burbank field	25	2 305	46 10
Ham, Roy			
24a E. E. Ingalls	400	400	8 00

RESIDENT INVOICE AND TAXES FOR THE YEAR 1934

NAME AND DESCRIPTION	VALUATION		TOTAL TAX
Hardie, Irene B. and John W.			
37a Joseph Blake	$2 200 00		
2 Cows	75	$2 275 00	$45 50
Hayes, Henry F.			
6i Over exemption	500		
1 Cow	45		
1 Neat stock	15	560	11 20
Heinlein, E. E.			
½a Levi Ayers	100		
2i Dana Eldridge	1 300		
Leroy Harris	700	2 100	42 00
Hersey, Abbie E.			
1a Camp and lot	1 000		
1a Hubbard camp	1 500	2 500	50 00
Hersey, Charles E.			
75i Farm	2 800		
20i Haley lot	150		
150a Piper lot	1 900		
Blacksmith shop	200		
20a Meadow	100		
1a Ann Haley lot	10		
74i John Haley	900		
1i J. M. Haley	1 500		
50a Pasture	1 250		
2 Horses	80		
3 Neat stock	80		
3 Cows	75	9 045	180 90
Hersey, D. J., Est.			
28a 8/15 Hersey farm	1 520		
8/15 Meadow	80	1 600	32 00
Hersey, Edwin C.			
75i Farm	1 200		
50i Copp lot	800		
1 Horse	60		
3 Cows	80	2 140	42 80

RESIDENT INVOICE AND TAXES FOR THE YEAR 1934

NAME AND DESCRIPTION	VALUATION		TOTAL TAX
Hersey, Everett U., Est.			
97ª Home place	$3 200 00		
40ɪ Severance	300	$3 500 00	$70 00
Hersey, Forrest W.			
1 Cow	25	25	50
Hersey, Frank A., heirs			
1a Home place	650		
15ɪ Foss lot	150		
30ª Blaisdell lot	1 100		
Camp and lot	1 000	2 900	58 00
Hersey, Mary P., heirs			
50ª Home place	700	700	14 00
Hersey, Otis A.			
124ɪ Home place	1 600		
95ɪ Pasture	1 600		
Log cabin and camp	1 200		
1 Cow	30		
2 Neat stock	50	4 480	89 60
Hilliard, Frank			
1a Home place	5 000	5 000	100 00
Hodgdon, C. H.			
4a Home place	2 200		
32a Remnant	300		
3a Levi Ladd	100		
1 Cow	20	2 620	52 40
Hodgdon, Forrest W.			
30ª Bradley Burleigh	660		
1 Horse	40		
4 Cows	160		
2 Neat stock	110		
Wood	120		
50a R. C. Glidden	300	1 390	27 80

RESIDENT INVOICE AND TAXES FOR THE YEAR 1934		
NAME AND DESCRIPTION	VALUATION	TOTAL TAX
Hodgdon, F. H.		
90ᵃ D. A. Wiggin	$2 500 00	
4 Cows	160	$2 660 00 $53 20
Hodgdon, Herbert F.		
85ᵃ Home place	1 400	
6ᵃ Palmer field	200	
6a Whitehouse field	100	
130a Lyford lot	660	
175a Pond lot	500	
15ᵃ Wood lot	50	2 910 58 20
Hodgdon, Jonathan, Est.		
110ᵃ Home place	1 500	1 500 30 00
Hodges, Milton		
Camp	600	600 12 00
Horner, George S.		
½a Store and house	2 000	
Island	200	
84ᵃ Dame lot	500	
Stewart lot	150	
Sullivan house	2 000	
Stock in trade	2 500	7 350 147 00
Howe, Carlton		
50a Elm house	1 200	
1 Horse	50	
1 Cow	30	1 280 25 60
Howe, Emma J.		
5ᵃ Home place	2 200	2 200 44 00
Howe, George F.		
½ Over exemption	800	800 16 00
Howe, Robert D.		
1½a Shop and lot	300	
2 Cows	85	385 7 70
Hoyt, Charles S.		
5a Home place	200	200 4 00

| RESIDENT INVOICE AND TAXES FOR THE YEAR 1934 | | |
NAME AND DESCRIPTION	VALUATION	TOTAL TAX
Hoyt, Frank E.			
2 Cows	$75 00	$75 00	$1 50
Hull, Clara B.			
3¼ Sam Piper	1 200	1 200	24 00
Hunt, Philip C.			
Camp	200	200	4 00
Hunter, Cora A.			
60a Ladd place	300		
130a George Fields	1 800	2 100	42 00
Hunter, Ernest M.			
50a Bald Peak Farm	3 200		
50¼ W. W. Treat	800		
20a Augustus Bean	100		
20a Mark Piper	600		
3 Horses	150		
4 Oxen	250		
3 Cows	110		
1 Neat stock	30	5 240	104 80
Jackson, Della			
50a C. W. Pinkham	1 000	1 000	20 00
Johnson, Bertha M.			
70a Wesley Canney	1 500		
5a C. H. Bennett	300		
4a Edith Craig	100	1 900	38 00
Johnson, Charles, Est.			
50a	2 700	2 700	54 00
Johnson, Charles W.			
3a Hunt field	200		
1 Horse	50		
11 Cows	440	690	13 80
Johnson, Louise P.			
Over exemption			
70a Amos Kimball	1 000		
Store	500		
2 Cows	80	1 580	31 60

| RESIDENT INVOICE AND TAXES FOR THE YEAR 1934 | | |
NAME AND DESCRIPTION	VALUATION	TOTAL TAX
Kane, Edward		
2ι Bungalow	$500 00	$500 00 $10 00
Keenan, Arthur		
16ι Jane Wiggin	1 600	
1 Cow	40	1 640 32 80
Kidd, Peter		
Small camp	150	150 3 00
Kling, Amy C.		
3ι Home place	2 200	
Gray Birches	1 000	3 200 64 00
Kramer, Rena		
1ι Walter Grant	2 000	
1 Cow	50	2 050 41 00
Kurth, John E.		
196a Henry Burleigh	2 900	
1 Horse	50	
2 Cows	70	
160 Fowl	120	3 140 62 80
Ladd, Levi W., Est.		
37a Home place	1 800	1 800 36 00
Lamprey, Carroll A.		
230a Lamprey farm	2 400	
143a Samoset Isl.	2 500	
80a Mountain lot	100	
18½a ½ Low lot	500	
18½a Alfreda Gridley	500	
2 Cows	50	
1 Horse	20	
1 Neat stock	15	6 085 121 70
Lamprey, Wilbur		
1½a Home place	550	
3 Cows	85	635 12 70

RESIDENT INVOICE AND TAXES FOR THE YEAR 1934

NAME AND DESCRIPTION	VALUATION		TOTAL TAX
Leary, John N.			
45ι Home place	$400 00	$400 00	$8 00
Leavitt, Lillian E.			
¼a W. Haley	1 000	1 000	20 00
Lord, Lizzie B.			
50ι Home place	1 000	1 000	20 00
Lugg, Eva D.			
3½a Over exemption	2 000	2 000	40 00
Marena, George H.			
C. E. Hersey camp	1 200		
5 George Hersey	600		
50a Charles Piper	200		
7a Albert Edgerly	700		
1 Cow	15	2 715	54 30
McDuffee, Gerald			
1 Cow	20		
Wood	72	92	1 84
McDuffee, Irving			
140a Home place	1 000		
2 Horses	125		
2 Cows	45		
5 Neat stock	190	1 360	27 20
McGee, Amy			
1a Knowles place	2 000	2 000	40 00
McIntire, Delma L.			
1 Cow	25	25	50
McIntire, Eunice			
14a Home place	1 500	1 500	30 00
McIntire, Lewis N.			
1a Home place	1 500		
125a J. M. Haley	400		
50a Canney lot	100		
1 Cow	30		
Store	300	2 330	46 60

NAME AND DESCRIPTION	VALUATION		TOTAL TAX
RESIDENT INVOICE AND TAXES FOR THE YEAR 1934			
McIntire, Selden			
170a Farm	$2 000 00		
3 Horses	170		
1 Ox	50		
4 Cows	85		
8 Neat stock	300		
20a Neal lot	200		
35a Canney lot	100		
64a Ham lot	200		
95a D. D. Wingate lot	600		
30a Young lot	200	$3 905 00	$78 10
McKean, Robert			
2a Home place	500		
20a Bickford lot	200		
1 Cow	20	720	14 40
Melvin Men's Club			
Club House	1 200	1 200	24 00
Merrifield, Nellie M.			
83a Home place	1 000		
1 Cow	35	1 035	20 70
Merritt, Rosie E. C.			
4a Home place	500	500	10 00
Milliner, Lillian, Est.			
70a John Haley	400	400	8 00
Minot, Mary			
25a ½ L. C. Canney	500	500	10 00
Morrill, Fred			
9a Home place	500	500	10 00
Morrill, Jean			
Camp - Samoset Isl.			
Lot No. 49	1 800	1 800	36 00
Morris, Hattie J.			
1a Home place	300	300	6 00
Moulton, Fred A.			
20a Home place	350	350	7 00

RESIDENT INVOICE AND TAXES FOR THE YEAR 1934

NAME AND DESCRIPTION	VALUATION		TOTAL TAX
Neal, Isaac N., Est.			
120a Farm	$2 750 00		
44ł Meadow	100		
80a Martin lot	500	$3 350 00	$67 00
Paige, Robert			
1a Home place	1 000		
3ł Upper Bay	200	1 200	24 00
Palmer, D. B.			
28a Drew lot	380		
10a Pine lot	300		
15ł A. W. Wiggin lot	160		
7a Clark lot	50		
30a Peavey lot	100	990	19 80
Pinkham, C. W., Est.			
House and store	2 000		
5ł A. L. Hersey	100		
100a Haley lot	650		
5a Meadow	50		
15ł Berry lot	200		
62½a Mt. Pleasant	300		
Stock in trade	2 000	5 300	106 00
Pinkham, Hattie M.			
Clyde Gould	700	700	14 00
Piper, Belle, Est.			
5ł House and store	2 000		
3a Jane Wiggin	300		
Stock in trade	800	3 100	62 00
Piper, Carrie S.			
110a Charles Lowe	1 800		
2 Oxen	100		
1 Cow	50	1 950	39 00
Piper, Charles G., heirs			
1a Geto lot	25	25	50

RESIDENT INVOICE AND TAXES FOR THE YEAR 1934

NAME AND DESCRIPTION	VALUATION		TOTAL TAX
Piper, John F.			
3a Home place	$500 00		
25ι J. M. Haley	300		
3 Cows	90	$890 00	$17 80
Poore, Edwin S.			
½a Camps	1 200	1 200	24 00
Pope, Grace H.			
Over exemption			
2ι Home place	4 000		
Blacksmith shop lot	100	4 100	82 00
Richardson, Alonzo L.			
and Eugene A.			
1a David Howe	600	600	12 00
Richardson, Anna A.			
7ι Home place	4 500		
25ι Canney lot	300		
150a Jones lot	800	5 600	112 00
Ridlon, Arthur L.			
1 Cow	30	30	60
Ridlon & Tucker			
Mirror Lake Garage	150	150	3 00
Roberts, George A.			
40ι Camp	420	420	8 40
Roghaar, Edward			
1 Horse	65	65	1 30
Rudolph, Roy			
1 Horse	60		
2 Cows	65	125	2 50
Sargent, Fred J.			
1a Home place	1 400	1 400	28 00
Sargent, Harold			
22a Part of Burleigh lot	75		
30a Richardson lot	150		
2 Cows	40		
2 Neat stock	100	365	7 30

RESIDENT INVOICE AND TAXES FOR THE YEAR 1934		
NAME AND DESCRIPTION	VALUATION	TOTAL TAX
Sargent, Jesse		
200ᵃ Home place	$1 000 00	
30a E. H. Deland	200	
33ᵃ Thompson lot	200	
1 Horse	60	
5 Cows	115	$1 575 00 $31 50
Schofield, Leigh		
Harry White Camp	1 800	1 800 36 00
Shannon, A. E.		
25ᵃ Home place	1 000	
New house	500	1 500 30 00
Shannon, Edward		
2 Horses	125	
2 Cows	42	167 3 34
Sheperd, Bertha		
Lot No. 56 Samoset Isl.	100	100 2 00
Sheperd, Leon F.		
1ᵃ Home place	2 000	
1a 2 Camps	1 200	
Pillsbnry lot	850	
Boats	100	4 150 83 00
Skinner, Walter		
25a Home place	1 200	1 200 24 00
Snow, John G.		
2 Horses	110	
2 Cows	60	170 3 40
Staples, Clarence		
10a George Piper	100	100 2 00
Stead, Harold		
50a Home place	2 400	
1 Horse	25	2 425 48 50
Stillings, Edward		
20ᵃ Chas. Horne	400	400 8 00
Stillings, Louise		
1a Bertha Sawyer	50	50 1 00

RESIDENT INVOICE AND TAXES FOR THE YEAR 1934

NAME AND DESCRIPTION	VALUATION		TOTAL TAX
Stillings, Roscoe			
1 Cow	$30 00	$30 00	$ 60
Straw, George D.			
½a A. H. Atherton	500		
50a John Stevens	700		
65a Frye lot	250		
35a Stevens lot	200		
30a Fernald lot	250		
6a Dame field	50		
1 Horse	20	1 970	39 40
Straw, Harry, Est.			
44a Home place	1 800		
3a Wiggin	300		
24a Wood lot	300		
1a Lucas field	50	2 450	49 00
Straw, Hattie			
1 Cow	35		
1 Neat stock	15	50	1 00
Swett, A. W., Est.			
10a Wood lot	300		
Camp	800	1 100	22 00
Thomas, Chester			
7a Annie Ladd	1 700		
1 Cow	15	1 715	34 30
Thomas, W. W.			
120a Home place	5 300		
83a Pasture	1 500		
27a Henry Hayes	500		
1 Horse	50		
5 Cows	150		
4 Neat stock	80	7 580	151 60
Thompson, Albert			
6a Wm. Swett	200	200	4 00
Thompson, Carrie			
160a R. Thompson	1 000		
110a Horne lot	700	1 700	34 00

RESIDENT INVOICE AND TAXES FOR THE YEAR 1934

NAME AND DESCRIPTION	VALUATION		TOTAL TAX
Thompson, John T.			
60a Home place	$1 500 00		
1a Baldwin place	200		
Camp and Island	300		
1 Boat	100	$2 100 00	$42 00
Thompson, Roy E.			
7a Horner field	400	400	8 00
Thompson, Simon B., heirs			
155a Home place	800	800	16 00
Thompson, Simon T.			
1 Horse	80		
4 Cows	95	175	3 50
Tuftonboro Grange			
3a Hall	1 000	1 000	20 00
Tupeck, Steve			
Over exemption	350		
1 Cow	40	390	7 80
Walker, Horace A.			
47a Mark Piper	500		
½a	100	600	12 00
Waterbury, Louis, Est.			
¾a The Pines	1 000	1 000	20 00
Watson, Alfred O.			
1a Home place	500		
5a Charles Davis	200	700	14 00
Watson, Gertrude E.			
8a Home place	1 200		
1 Horse	50		
1 Cow	22	1 272	25 44
Watson, Russell			
1a Camp	250	250	5 00
Welch, George			
1a Ben Stokes	1 200		
40a D. D. Wingate	150		
50a Hersey lot	650		
5a Straw lot	100		
1 Cow	22	2 122	42 44

RESIDENT INVOICE AND TAXES FOR THE YEAR 1934

NAME AND DESCRIPTION	VALUATION		TOTAL TAX
Welch, Jane			
2½ Store	$500 00		
1a Addie Ham	40		
Stock in trade	300	$840 00	$16 80
Welch, Maurice			
Garage	75	75	1 50
Welch, Oren			
24½ E. E. Ingalls	300		
1 Cow	35	335	6 70
Wentworth, Frank, heirs			
30a Peavey lot	300	300	6 00
West, Addie			
90a Home place	1 400		
1 Horse	50		
5 Cows	170	1 620	32 40
West, Lawrence P.			
62½a Mt. Pleasant	300	300	6 00
Whedon, Annie S.			
22a Ed. Hersey	500		
2/15 Meadow	20		
2/15 Hersey farm	380		
½a Home place	700		
20a Levi Ayers	130	1 730	34 60
Whedon, Oscar A.			
1 Cow	25	25	50
Whitten, Carrie G.			
130a J. A. Wiggin	300		
15a Home place	600		
1 Horse	50		
6 Cows	180	1 130	22 60
Whitten, John R.			
100a Shore Acres	6 000		
2 Horses	125		
1 Cow	40		
2 Neat stock	50	6 215	124 30

RESIDENT INVOICE AND TAXES FOR THE YEAR 1934

NAME AND DESCRIPTION	VALUATION		TOTAL TAX
Whitten, Joseph W.			
40ᴸ Elisha Woodworth	$800 00		
100ᴸ Home place	1 500		
25ᵃ Everett Hersey lot	40		
2 Horses	75		
13 Cows	380		
1 Neat stock	25	$2 820 00	$56 40
Wiggin, Harold I.			
½ᵃ Home place	400	400	8 00
Wilcox, Nell H.			
1ᵃ New camp	3 500	3 500	70 00
Willand, W. P.			
60ᵃ Home place	1 000	1 000	20 00
Williams, Nellie M.			
½ᵃ Home place	700	700	14 00
Williams, Roger L.			
77ᵃ J. M. Haley	1 500	1 500	30 00
Winnipesaukee Motor Craft Co.			
1ᵃ Land and buildings	4 600		
1 Boat	100		
Stock in trade	100		
Machinery	300	5 100	102 00
Woodmancy, Florence I.			
50ᵃ John R. Wendall	1 800	1 800	36 00
Woodmancy, H. A.			
4 Cows	150		
2 Neat stock	40	190	3 80
Woodward, H. M.			
1ᵃ Camp	1 500	1 500	30 00
Young, Lura			
63ᵃ Home place	700	700	14 00
Young, Royal P.			
46ᵃ Home place	1 000		
230 Fowl	197 50	1 197 50	23 95

INVENTORY

OF THE NON-RESIDENT TAXPAYERS

OF THE TOWN OF TUFTONBORO

NON - RESIDENT INVOICE AND TAXES FOR THE YEAR 1934

NAME AND DESCRIPTION	VALUATION		TOTAL TAX
Abbott, Charles W.			
¾a Fred Wiggin	$900 00	$900 00	$18 00
Abbott, William			
6a Gertrude Grant	150	150	3 00
Adams, F. Mildred			
Lot No. 5 Samoset Isl.	1 000	1 000	20 00
Allen, Howard S.			
1a E. B. Edgerly	1 000	1 000	20 00
Allstrom, Anna			
Camp - Beech Pond	400	400	8 00
Allstrom, Emma C.			
Camp - Beech Pond	400	400	8 00
Anderson, Mr., c/o Thos. Bray			
1 Boat	100	100	2 00
Anderson, Herbert			
½a E. B. Edgerly	1 000	1 000	20 00
Arnold, Sarah L.			
5a Part Whortleberry Isl.	300	300	6 00
Babbitt, A. B.			
3a E. B. Edgerly	800	800	16 00
Bald Peak Country Club			
650a Lots 68 - 69 - 70			
72 - 73 - 74 - 75	4 200		
1 Boat	1 800		
25a Gordon lot	3 000		
35a Horne lot	2 000		
½a Campbell lot	1 000	12 000	240 00

NON-RESIDENT INVOICE AND TAXES FOR THE YEAR 1934

NAME AND DESCRIPTION	VALUATION		TOTAL TAX
Banfield, Alberta P.			
Camp and lot	$1 200 00		
1 Boat	600	$1 800 00	$36 00
Banfield, Laura			
4ᵃ Fay Camp, Birch			
and Squirrel Islands	2 000		
70ᵃ George Morrison	2 000	4 000	80 00
Barber, Isabel D.			
6ᵃ W. F. Plant	30 000		
2 Boats	2 800	32 800·	656 00
Barnard, Paul L.			
1 Boat	100	100	2 00
Bassett, Charles S.			
136a Farm	1 000	1 000	20 00
Beacham, Darius			
48a J. H. Willand	250	250	5 00
Bent, George W., Est.			
85a Dodge pasture	500	500	10 00
Bentley, Walter			
1 Boat	200	200	4 00
Bernard, M. C., heirs			
7a Camp and lot	4 200	4 200	84 00
Betchley, E. Gertrude			
Camp, Hersey pasture	1 800	1 800	36 00
Beverly National Bank			
1a Whittle camp	5 000		
1 Boat	400	5 400	108 00
Bibeault, Philip			
1 Boat	2 500	2 500	50 00
Bisbee, Chester A.			
10a George O. Bean	50	50	1 00
Bixby, H. O.			
5a Camp and lot	3 500	3 500	70 00
Black, Margaret A. and Henry			
140a John Neal	3 200	3 200	64 00

NON - RESIDENT INVOICE AND TAXES FOR THE YEAR 1934

NAME AND DESCRIPTION	VALUATION		TOTAL TAX
Blackstone, H. A.			
300ı Part of Cow Isl. $12 000 00			
Devon Island	800	$12 800 00	$256 00
Blaisdell, Mark B.			
Camp Wigwam			
C. H. Young	700	700	14 00
Blount, John G.			
30ı Camp and lot	3 200		
1 Boat	300	3 500	70 00
Blount, John G., Jr.			
Camp and lot	2 000	2 000	40 00
Boody, Forrest			
4ı N. Berry	500	500	10 00
Bookholz, Ethel			
50ı Fanny Horne	1 200	1 200	24 00
Borden, C. H.			
½ı Ray Wiggin	800	800	16 00
Bosher, Hannah			
170ı C. A. Batchelder	4 500	4 500	90 00
Boston, Y. M. C. A.			
66ı Sandy Island	7 000		
110ı Frank Blake	12 000		
1 Boat	700	19 700	394 00
Bowker, H. D.			
1ı Camp and boathouse	3 000		
1 Boat	1 500	4 500	90 00
Breen, D. J.			
1 Boat	750	750	15 00
Brehm, E. P.			
2 Boats	2 600	2 600	52 00
Brennar, Thomas			
Camp	800	800	16 00
Brickley, James			
1 Boat	100	100	2 00

NON - RESIDENT INVOICE AND TAXES FOR THE YEAR 1934		
NAME AND DESCRIPTION	VALUATION	TOTAL TAX
Bridgden, George I.		
1a Sarah White	$1 800 00	$1 800 00	$36 00
Briggs, George S.		
7a M. E. Atkins	3 500		
1 Boat	750	4 250	85 00
Briggs, M. L.		
21a Camp and lot	600	600	12 00
Brim, Orville		
3a E. R. Whitten	4 000	4 000	80 00
Britton, W. J.		
30a Fay lot	50	50	1 00
Brock, Elbert H.		
103a Baldwin place	5 300	5 300	106 00
Brophy, Wm. S.		
1 Boat	2 700	2 700	54 00
Brower, William L.		
4a Camp and lot	1 600	1 600	32 00
Brown, Bernard		
Lot on Beech Pond	100	100	2 00
Browne, Walter A.		
Camp and lots 54 and		
55 Samoset Isl.	1 300	1 300	26 00
Bulfinch, H. C., Est.		
Camp and lot	2 000	2 000	40 00
Bulfinch, Mildred		
Wee Hoose	400	400	8 00
Burleigh, H. S., Est.		
Meadow	100	100	2 00
Burleigh, H. T.		
12a Narrows	700	700	14 00
Bushnell, William M.		
5a Rollin Jones, Sr.	18 000		
2 Boats	3 500	21 500	430 00

NON - RESIDENT INVOICE AND TAXES FOR THE YEAR 1934		
NAME AND DESCRIPTION	VALUATION	TOTAL TAX
Butler, Ethel M.		
Camp and lot	$1 500 00 $1 500 00	$30 00
Butler, W. O.		
65a J. W. Haley	800 800	16 00
Cain, John J.		
⅓a Fred Wiggin	300 300	6 00
Callahan, Susan P.		
5ᵢ G. T. Dudley	4 000 4 000	80 00
Cameron, F. M.		
Camp and lot	600 600	12 00
Campbell, C. I., Est.		
Camp and lot	3 000 3 000	60 00
Carleton, Earl		
Camp lot, C. O. Dore	300 300	6 00
Carlton, Walter		
½a Camp on Beech Pond 500	500	10 00
Carpenter, Frank		
14ᵢ J. M. Welch	1 000 1 000	20 00
Carpenter, Ralph G.		
50a Capitola Tyler	2 200 2 200	44 00
Case, Walter S.		
1 Boat	1 500 1 500	30 00
Caulfield, A. J.		
6a John Fox	2 500 2 500	50 00
Chandler, H. P.		
130a Caverly farm	3 500 3 500	70 00
Cheney, A.		
1 Boat	100 100	2 00
Chevalier, J. F.		
100a J. Willand	1 350 1 350	27 00
Chevalier, S. M.		
1a Jas. Horner	1 500 1 500	30 00

NON - RESIDENT INVOICE AND TAXES FOR THE YEAR 1934

NAME AND DESCRIPTION	VALUATION		TOTAL TAX
Clark, Alexander			
28a Upper Bay	$2 000 00		
¼a Bean house	100	$2 100 00	$42 00
Clark, Paul F.			
¾a George Straw	2 000	2 000	40 00
Clow, Dr. F. E.			
Bennett camp and lot	300	300	6 00
Clow & Rollins			
33a Bean lot	150	150	3 00
Collier, John			
½a 2 Camps	3 000	3 000	60 00
Collins, John M.			
½a E. T. Westcott	2 000		
Jackson lot	450		
5a J. M. Haley	300		
1 Boat	1 000	3 750	75 00
Conant, Mary B.			
4a Camp	6 000	6 000	120 00
Condit, Sears			
3a Blazo place	3 000		
20a Copp field	1 500	4 500	90 00
Connelley, Aloysius			
⅓a Fred Wiggin	300	300	6 00
Craig, John W.			
5a Bowman field	300	300	6 00
Craig, Robert B.			
⅔a Camp Beech Pond	400	400	8 00
Crane, Eleanor W.			
Willand Island	100	100	2 00
Crane, William N.			
3a Horace McIntire	1 800		
1 Boat	100	1 900	38 00
Cummings, E. A.			
½a Theo. Hunt camp	200	200	4 00

NON-RESIDENT INVOICE AND TAXES FOR THE YEAR 1934		
NAME AND DESCRIPTION	VALUATION	TOTAL TAX
Cummings, F. E.		
Camp and lot	$1 200 00	$1 200 00	$24 00
Dane, Ernest B.		
Bennett mill site	250	250	5 00
Daniels, Frank		
2ı Banfield Piper	200	200	4 00
D'Arcy, Gerald J.		
14ı Clara R. Stidham	3 500		
25ı Manly Brett	500		
1 Boat	1 000	5 000	100 00
Davis, Dr. % R. Goodrich		
1 Boat	200	200	4 00
Davis, Bertha R.		
C. H. Young	700	700	14 00
Davis, Paul A.		
1a Camp and lot	2 000	2 000	40 00
Davy, Alice M.		
Pleasant & Bellevue Isls.	500	500	10 00
Dickey, Everett E.		
Tonawanda	2 000	2 000	40 00
Doe, Andrew F.		
150a Frank Doe farm	4 500		
3 Cows	105		
4 Neat stock	110	4 715	94 30
Doe, Harry C.		
Camp - E. B. Edgerly	3 000	3 000	60 00
Doe & Stackpole		
5ı Geto lot	100	100	2 00
Dolloff, George S.		
Camp on Beech Pond	500	500	10 00
Dore, Charles O., heirs		
60a Augustus Wiggin	1 500	1 500	30 00

NON - RESIDENT INVOICE AND TAXES FOR THE YEAR 1934		
NAME AND DESCRIPTION	VALUATION	TOTAL TAX
Dore, S. S.		
35a McDuffee	$300 00	$300 00	$6 00
Dore, W. P.		
Hanson mill	500	
10a Pine lot	100	
40a Levi Brown	200	800	16 00
Doremus, Widmer		
10a Frank Piper	3 500	3 500	70 00
Drown, Edwin S.		
E. R. Whitten	3 000	3 000	60 00
Duane, J. M.		
1 Boat	1 000	1 000	20 00
Dudley, G. T.		
90a Everett Horne	800	800	16 00
Dunbar, Bonnie L.		
1 Boat	750	750	15 00
Dunsford, Samuel		
15a H. F. Hurlburt	22 000	
5 Boats	6 300	28 300	566 00
Durland, Eula L.		
10a John A. Edgerly	2 000	2 000	40 00
Eaton, Izora G.		
Lot No. 59 Samoset Isl.	100	100	2 00
Edgar, L.		
1 Boat	3 500	3 500	70 00
Eldridge, Dana		
30a A. W. Swett	300	
½a Home place	600	900	18 00
Elmore, Carl H.		
Bear Isl. lot No. 18	300	300	6 00
Emery, Howard		
½a	500	
14a S. J. Thompson	200	700	14 00

NON - RESIDENT INVOICE AND TAXES FOR THE YEAR 1934		
NAME AND DESCRIPTION	VALUATION	TOTAL TAX
Farrington, W. M.		
2ι Cottage	$1 400 00	$1 400 00	$28 00
Felker, Henry W., Est.		
30ι D. J. Brown	600	600	12 00
Fernald, H. E., heirs		
Davis House	1 700	1 700	34 00
Fleck, William C., Est.		
Dr. Libby lot	700	700	14 00
Flint, Harley A.		
1a Camp and lot	2 500	2 500	50 00
Foederer, P. E.		
Horn point	2 000	2 000	40 00
Foster. Ann D.		
4ι I. S. Wiggin	2 500	2 500	50 00
Fox, Alice and Lillian		
Tea Room	1 000	1 000	20 00
Fox, J. E., Est.		
95ι Asa Fox	3 500	3 500	70 00
French, George B., heirs		
325ι ½ int.		
J. French lot	5 000	5 000	100 00
French, Martha, Est.		
325ι ½ Int.		
J. French lot	5 000	5 000	100 00
Fulton, Caroline, Est.		
½ Fulton Est.	1 000	1 000	20 00
Furst, W. S., Est.		
½a Camp lot	500		
9a Everett Hersey	300	800	16 00
Gardner, Nellie B.		
20ι	200	200	4 00
Gardner, W. A. A.		
1a	1 000	1 000	20 00
George, Ruth Hall		
1a Camp and lot	1 600	1 600	32 00
Glidden, Amelia		
20a J. Glidden	300	300	6 00

NON-RESIDENT INVOICE AND TAXES FOR THE YEAR 1934		
NAME AND DESCRIPTION	VALUATION	TOTAL TAX
Glidden, Josie E.		
20a Goldsmith lot	$400 00 $400 00	$8 00
Golding, Philip S.		
Jemima Dore	300 300	6 00
Goodell, George A.		
½a Camp and lot	1 200 1 200	24 00
Goodwin, J. Frank		
15a Jane Wiggin	150	
12a I. S. Wiggin	150 300	6 00
Gordon, Albert S.		
1a Camp and lot	1 800 1 800	36 00
Goss, Leroy		
Stock in trade	125 125	2 50
Gram, Emma		
Camp and lots 22		
23-24 Bear Island	1 500 1 500	30 00
Grebenstein, Susan		
C. H. Bennett	2 500 2 500	50 00
Greene, George W., Tr.		
40a Whortleberry Isl.	1 500 1 500	30 00
Gucker, Frank T.		
Boathouse	350	
1 Boat	200 550	11 00
Gucker, Louise O.		
1a ½ Fulton Est.	1 000 1 000	20 00
Gulf Refining Co.		
6 Gasolene pumps		
and tanks	450 450	9 00
Gustafson, Elias		
40a Camp Beech Pond	600 600	12 00
Haigh, Robert and Elizabeth		
E. B. Edgerly	500 500	10 00
Haley, Abel		
20a Pasture	100 100	2 00

NON - RESIDENT INVOICE AND TAXES FOR THE YEAR 1934		
NAME AND DESCRIPTION	VALUATION	TOTAL TAX
Haley, Charles W.		
22ı Pasture Beech Pond $100 00	$100 00	$2 00
Hall, Carl A.		
Frank Speare	1 400	1 400	28 00
Hannon, John A.		
Fanny Kimball	250	250	5 00
Hanson, Mary E.		
Part Whortleberry Island 100	100	2 00
Hardon, Corrine T.		
14ı Baxter place	2 200	2 200	44 00
Harris, Leroy A.		
C. O. Dore	700	700	14 00
Hatch, Georgia		
2a Andrew Thomas	1 200	1 200	24 00
Haven, Sarah K.		
Camp and lot	2 500	2 500	50 00
Haydecke, Franklin		
2 Boats	1 800	1 800	36 00
Hayes, Ellen, Est.		
3ı W. W. Thomas	500	500	10 00
Hayes, Rosa P.		
6ı W. W. Thomas	1 000	1 000	20 00
Hersey, Austin		
1a Home place of		
Frank Staples	600	600	12 00
Hersey, Estelle M., ·Est.		
Camp and lot	1 000	1 000	20 00
Hersey, Virgil P.		
140a A. L. Hersey	1 000		
Camp	300	1 300	26 00
Hesslor, F. D.		
½a Jesse Welch	6 000	6 000	120 00

NON-RESIDENT INVOICE AND TAXES FOR THE YEAR 1934

NAME AND DESCRIPTION	VALUATION		TOTAL TAX
Hesslor, H. J.			
Luddy camp	$7 000 00		
1 Boat	800	$7 800 00	$156 00
Hesslor, H. J. and others			
Camp lot	700	700	14 00
Hitchings, Eben E.			
Camp - Hersey pasture	2 500	2 500	50 00
Hodgdon, Ray F.			
7a Haley lot	100	100	2 00
Hodkins, Woodbury			
135a Nat. Neal place	1 500	1 500	30 00
Hopewell, Henry C.			
1 Boat	1 600	1 600	32 00
Horne, Charles A.			
31a Remick place	6 200		
Rockaway camp	1 500	7 700	154 00
Horn, Ralph			
50a T. B. Horn	500	500	10 00
Howard, G. K.			
100a Mountain lot	500	500	10 00
Huber, Margaret O.			
Narrows	6 000	6 000	120 00
Hull, George I.			
140a Wm. Bixby	6 000	6 000	120 00
Hull, Laura			
½a J. A. Edgerly	1 000	1 000	20 00
Hull, Manton			
1 Boat	100	100	2 00
Humphrey, G. B., Est.			
100a Windleblo	4 800	4 800	96 00
Hunt, Eva			
7a Pasture	200	200	4 00
Hunter, Mrs. A. A.			
2a W. W. Thomas	3 000	3 000	60 00

NON - RESIDENT INVOICE AND TAXES FOR THE YEAR 1934		
NAME AND DESCRIPTION	VALUATION	TOTAL TAX
Hunter, J. S.		
1 Boat	$200 00	$200 00	$4 00
Hurlburt, Fanny E.		
95ı Hurlburt farm	14 000	
Small camp	1 000	15 000	300 00
Hurlburt, H. F., Jr.		
Harry Hurlburt camp	2 500	2 500	50 00
Idlewild, Camp		
220a Part of Cow Isl.	14 000	
Boats	200	14 200	284 00
Jackson, Florence S.		
Camp and lot	1 400	
24ı J. M. Haley	350	1 750	35 00
James, Philip		
1 Boat	200	200	4 00
Johnstone, Wm. J.		
100ı No. 9	700	700	14 00
Jones, Maud R.		
½a W. S. Furst	700	700	14 00
Keigwin, A. E.		
47ı Horace McIntire	3 000	3 000	60 00
Kells, J. C.		
Camp lot, A. Thompson	275	275	5 50
Kennington, H. C., agent		
Walker Hotel	2 000	2 000	40 00
Kennington, Mrs. H. C.		
2a Mazuz field	1 000	1 000	20 00
Krey, Minnie E.		
44ı J. R. Wendall	7 000	
1 Boat	200	7 200	144 00
Ladd, Annie P.		
60ı Pasture	400	400	8 00

NON-RESIDENT INVOICE AND TAXES FOR THE YEAR 1934		
NAME AND DESCRIPTION	VALUATION	TOTAL TAX
Ladd, Mary P.		
30a Harvey Ladd	$1 000 00 $1 000 00	$20 00
Lahtie, Matthew and		
George Rockwell		
2ι Dr. Bradford camp	700 700	14 00
LeBlanc, Joseph		
and Lucy Patch		
97a Kate Thompson	1 000	
1 Cow	40 1 040	20 80
LeFavre, Wm. O.		
50ι Everett Horn	4 000	
1a Beech Pond	100	
67a Horne lot	300 4 400	88 00
Levy, Maurice A.		
½a H. F. Hodgdon	600 600	12 00
Libby, H. F., Est.		
20ι Narrows	2 000	
8a I. S. Wiggin	1 000	
150a Banfield Piper	2 000	
40a V. P. Hersey	500 5 500	110 00
Libby, Norman		
25a	200 200	4 00
Lilley, Edwin S., Est.		
11a Ragged Isl.	4 000	
1 Boat	500 4 500	90 00
Litchfield, J. Q.		
Camp - Merrymount	1 900 1 900	38 00
Little, Clara B.		
1a Lot 13, Bear Isl.	400 400	8 00
Little, Laura R. & C. C.		
1a Lots 14 and 15		
Bear Isl.	800 800	16 00

| NON-RESIDENT INVOICE AND TAXES FOR THE YEAR 1934 | | |
NAME AND DESCRIPTION	VALUATION	TOTAL TAX
Loomis, Paul, Est.		
2a 2 Camps and lot 43		
Bear Isl.	$2 500 00 $2 500 00	$50 00
Lord, Frank S.		
33⅓a Lot 56 ⅓ int.	300 300	6 00
Loring, Adelaide S.		
12a Camp and lot	3 000 3 000	60 00
Loring, Charles A.		
14a E. E. Fall	2 200 2 200	44 00
Low, E. F.		
1 Boat	400 400	8 00
Lynch, Harriet L.		
1a Galloup camp	5 000 5 000	100 00
Lyndol, Annie F.		
Camp and lot	6 000	
1 Boat	500 6 500	130 00
Lyon, W. Wallace		
2 Boats	1 700 1 700	34 00
Malcolm, Estelle		
Lot Bear Isl.	400 400	8 00
Mallett, Chas. E		
C. O. Dore	600 600	12 00
Manchester, Florence		
3a Frank Blake	1 500 1 500	30 00
Marden, Mary H.		
2a Alfred Hodgkins	1 000 1 000	20 00
Marvin, Agnes		
26a Francis Straw	2 000	
Shore lot	100 2 100	42 00
Matson, Hilma M.		
Camp and lot		
Whortleberry Isl.	500 500	10 00

NON - RESIDENT INVOICE AND TAXES FOR THE YEAR 1934

NAME AND DESCRIPTION	VALUATION		TOTAL TAX
McDougall, Edward			
8ı Everett Wiggin	$25 000 00		
8ı J. M. Welch	1 000		
26a A. W. Swett	2 600		
1 Boat	1 000	$29 600 00	$592 00
McGaw, John			
1a Levi Ferguson	300	300	6 00
Meader, Harry H.			
1a Cottage	2 000	2 000	40 00
Meehan, Alice K.			
Seavey place	800	800	16 00
Merrow, Parker N.			
100a C. E. Ham	800	800	16 00
Meyer, Max H.			
60a I. S. Wiggin	3 000	3 000	60 00
Miller, Glenna			
10a Holmes farm	3 000	3 000	60 00
Montgomery, W. B.			
1a Narrows	5 000	5 000	100 00
Moore, Alta			
Camp and land			
G. B. Humphrey	1 200	1 200	24 00
Morrison, A. H.			
1a E. R. Whitten	3 000		
1 Boat	500	3 500	70 00
Morrison, George W.			
10a Melvin Island	100	100	2 00
Morse, George D., Jr.			
1a E. B. Edgerly	1 500	1 500	30 00
Murch, Thomas			
35a John Waldron	300	300	6 00
National City Bank of Lynn			
18a L. V. Grover Isl.	4 500	4 500	90 00

NON-RESIDENT INVOICE AND TAXES FOR THE YEAR 1934

NAME AND DESCRIPTION	VALUATION		TOTAL TAX
Neal, John, heirs			
12a Meadow	$25 00	$25 00	$ 50
Nelson, Alfred S.			
Camp, Beech Pond	500	500	10 00
Nelson, Warren			
40a Asa Beacham	500	500	10 00
Newell, Bessie			
Camp lot	300		
1 Boat	150	450	9 00
Newman, Jennie			
3a Lizzie Lord	500	500	10 00
Ossipee Valley Land Corporation			
60a A. K. Roberts	300		
50a Benj. Ilam	200		
300a H. McDuffee	1 500		
800a Lots 35 - 37 - 39 - 52			
53 - 54 - 55 - 57 - 58 - 59			
60 - 61 - 62 - 63 - 64 - 65	2 250		
35a Anna Neal	75		
40a E. McDuffee	100		
30a 2/3 Jane Moody	600		
15a Ernest Deland	75		
75a Moulton lot	75		
25a Guppy lot	200		
Wood	2 800	8 175	163 50
Paige, Sydney			
1a I. S. Wiggin	1 200	1 200	24 00
Parker, Alfred B.			
64a Sandy Knoll	1 600	1 600	32 00
Parsons, Annie M.			
2 Camps Bear Island	1 200	1 200	24 00
Peavey, Willard R.			
25a E. Peavey	350	350	7 00

NON-RESIDENT INVOICE AND TAXES FOR THE YEAR 1934		
NAME AND DESCRIPTION	VALUATION	TOTAL TAX
Pigott, Thomas		
C. Young	$800 00	$800 00	$16 00
Piper, Fred L.		
1a Thatcher Piper	1 800	1 800	36 00
Plant, H. S.		
1 Boat	600	600	12 00
Plant, Thomas G.		
50a Robert Lamprey	1 700	1 700	34 00
Porter, Henry P.		
½a Jane Wiggin	2 000	2 000	40 00
Preble, Roger W.		
and Myrtle D.		
½a Camp Dolloff	300	300	6 00
Priggin, George		
40a George Moody	1 500		
20a Jane Moody	300	1 800	36 00
Public Service Co. of N. H.		
6 Miles H. T. line	15 000	15 000	300 00
Qua, Clara F.		
1a C. O. Dore	500	500	10 00
Quigley, Joseph C.		
C. H. Young	700		
1 Boat	200	900	18 00
Rau, Albert C.		
¼ C. I. Campbell	1 000	1 000	20 00
Reed, Walter A.		
3a Camp and lot	1 500	1 500	30 00
Renaud, Ralph E.		
E. R. Whitten	4 000	4 000	80 00
Rice, Leonard		
½a Camp and lot	1 300	1 300	26 00
Richardson, F. M.		
88a Daniel Libby	1 600	1 600	32 00

NON - RESIDENT INVOICE AND TAXES FOR THE YEAR 1934

NAME AND DESCRIPTION	VALUATION		TOTAL TAX
Ricker, Bertha			
20a J. L. Goldsmith	$150 00		
30a Lillian Bean	50		
1a A. K. Roberts	25	$225 00	$4 50
Rowe, Charles			
Fanny Kimball	100	100	2 00
Sams, E. M.			
2 Boats	2 100	2 100	42 00
Sanborn, Dr. Mary N.			
Echo Island	900	900	18 00
Sawyer, Fred H.			
10a Sawyer's Point	6 000	6 000	120 00
Saxton, Charles A.			
Lots 44 - 45 Samoset	2 500	2 500	50 00
Schweitzer, Adele			
10a Hitchins camp	8 000		
1 Boat	500	8 500	170 00
Senior, Helen G.			
½a Camp and lot, E. Gordon	1 700	1 700	34 00
Severance, Walter			
20a 2 Pastures	200	200	4 00
Shaw, Samuel			
Phinney camp	5 000		
2a Pillsbury camp	3 700		
2a Welles	1 000	9 700	194 00
Shell Eastern Petroleum Products, Inc.			
3 Pumps and tanks	300	300	6 00
Shohl, A. T.			
Clara Stidham	1 500	1 500	30 00
Sleigh, W. B.			
Merrymount	1 400	1 400	28 00

| NON-RESIDENT INVOICE AND TAXES FOR THE YEAR 1934 | | |
NAME AND DESCRIPTION	VALUATION	TOTAL TAX
Sliter, Ethel		
Merrymount	$1 400 00	
Small camp	400	
Lots 16 & 17 Samoset	400	$2 200 00 $44 00
Smith, E. H., Est.		
Beech Pond	700	700 14 00
Smith, Harold W.		
Camp, Beech Pond	700	700 14 00
Smith, Jesse M.		
20a J. A. Edgerly	2 700	2 700 54 00
Smith, Philip S.		
E. S. Poor	4 000	
1 Boat	500	
44a A. W. Swett	500	5 000 100 00
Sparks, Ralph M.		
Merrymount	1 500	1 500 30 00
Sparks & Speare		
1 Boat	500	500 10 00
Speare, Frank P.		
Store Island	50	
100a D. D. Wingate	3 400	
25a Wm. Straw	500	
1 Horse	50	4 000 80 00
Speare, Katherine V.		
25a Merrymount	3 000	3 000 60 00
Stack, Ena D.		
1a Elijah Canney	3 500	3 500 70 00
Stadie, Dr. W. C.		
1 Boat	200	200 4 00
Standard Oil Co.		
27 Pumps and tanks	1 800	1 800 36 00
Staples, Frank		
15a Clark lot	150	
10a Pine lot	200	350 7 00
Stevens, Henry		
5a Narrows	500	500 10 00

NON - RESIDENT INVOICE AND TAXES FOR THE YEAR 1934

NAME AND DESCRIPTION	VALUATION		TOTAL TAX
Stevens, Hubert			
Camp lot	$200 00	$200 00	$4 00
Stillings, F. O.			
14i Veazey lot	100		
60i Bickford lot	500	600	12 00
Sweet, Maria L.			
2i J. M. Haley	200	200	4 00
Swift, Bernice			
Pine Tree Island	500	500	10 00
Sylvester, C. J.			
Fanny Kimball	150	150	3 00
Tapley, I. M.			
1 Boat	150	150	3 00
Tarbell, Luther L.			
1a Evelyn Brown	500	500	10 00
Taylor, Dr. W. D.			
2 Boats	1 000	1 000	20 00
Teague, Walter D. and Cecil F.			
25a J. A. Edgerly	400		
26i Carrie Piper	5 500	5 900	118 00
Temple, R. L.			
C. H. Young	1 000	1 000	20 00
Texas Co., The			
2 Gasolene pumps and tanks	150	150	3 00
Thompson, Carrie S.			
70i Moulton lot	250	250	5 00
Thompson, W. A., heirs			
6a Daniel Horne	500	500	10 00
Thompson, William, heirs			
100a Wm. Thompson	2 800	2 800	56 00
Thompson, Trickey & Horne			
96i Hersey point	8 700	8 700	174 00
Tolland, P. J.			
C. O. Dore	400	400	8 00

NON-RESIDENT INVOICE AND TAXES FOR THE YEAR 1934

NAME AND DESCRIPTION	VALUATION		TOTAL TAX
Tomb, John M.			
E. R. Whitten	$5 000 00		
1 Boat	300	$5 300 00	$106 00
Torney, Franklin L.			
Keenan camp	800		
1 Boat	100	900	18 00
Town of Berwick, Me.			
25a ⅓ Lena Clark Est.	500	500	10 00
Towne, Lockwood J.			
1a E. R. Whitten	1 000	1 000	20 00
Turner, Harry C.			
7a C. H. Young	1 500	1 500	30 00
Turrill, Donald J.			
½ Camp and lot			
Hersey pasture	1 700	1 700	34 00
Tuttle, Eugene			
6a Rollins place	900	900	18 00
Tyler, H. W.			
Horace McIntire	900	900	18 00
Updegraff, R. D.			
185a George Welch	3 000		
Camp lot	300	3 300	66 00
Van Horsen, Ella F.			
2½a O. Richardson	1 200	1 200	24 00
Vose, E. M.			
¼a Charles Parsons	800	800	16 00
Walker, H. A.			
1 Boat	500	500	10 00
Waner, W. F.			
1 Boat	400	400	8 00
Waters, Isabel			
1a Theo. Hunt	1 000	1 000	20 00

NON - RESIDENT INVOICE AND TAXES FOR THE YEAR 1934		
NAME AND DESCRIPTION	VALUATION	TOTAL TAX
Weeks, Walter		
67ᴀ Lot 56 ⅔ int.	$600 00	
200ᴀ McDuffee lot	800	$1 400 00 $28 00
Welch, Wm.		
Lot, E. M. Hunter	800	800 16 00
Wheeler, Percy G.		
Bonny View	800	
1 Boat	500	1 300 26 00
White Mt. Power Co.		
21 Miles line	14 000	14 000 280 00
Whitney, Carrie G.		
13ᴀ J. H. Piper	1 000	1 000 20 00
Whiting, Arthur D.		
½a Wingate Cove	1 300	1 300 26 00
Whittemore, F. L.		
1ᴀ Luther Lee	1 200	1 200 24 00
Wiggin, Fred A.		
30ᴀ Big house	3 200	
2ᴀ Cottage	1 000	
Stable camp	1 000	5 200 104 00
Wiggin, George E.		
100ᴀ Pasture	1 000	1 000 20 00
Wilcox, Cara		
8ᴀ Wawbeek road	800	
2 Camp lots	300	1 100 22 00
Wilder, Clara T.		
50ᴀ L. Thompson	150	150 3 00
Willand, Howard		
44ᴀ Pasture	500	500 10 00
Willard, Iva M.		
1ᴀ Henry Durgin	2 500	
Elletta Durgin camp	1 200	3 700 74 00
Willis, Charles and Celia		
Edith Craig	500	500 10 00

NON-RESIDENT INVOICE AND TAXES FOR THE YEAR 1934

NAME AND DESCRIPTION	VALUATION		TOTAL TAX
Winchester, Maria			
23a Farm Island	$2 000 00	$2 000 00	$40 00
Wood, Arthur A.			
3a Charles G. Piper	500	500	10 00
Wood, Carl A., Est.			
1a Grace I. Wood	1 000	1 000	20 00
Wood, Edna			
Camp Powhatan			
C. H. Young	700	700	14 00
Wood, Harry			
15a Nat. Neal	1 000	1 000	20 00
Woodward, Percy			
E. R. Whitten	5 500		
179a J. A. Brackett	4 000	9 500	190 00
Wylie, John H.			
Camp, Beech Pond	600	600	12 00
Wylie, William			
Lot, Beech Pond	100	100	2 00
Wyman, Louis			
1 Boat	500	500	10 00
Yeaton, Janet			
Helen's Island	100		
Lot No. 23	100	200	4 00
Young, Chas. H.			
2 Camps	1 400		
1 Boat	100	1 500	30 00

Vital Statistics

For

1934

Marriages Registered in the Town of Tuftonboro, N. H., for the year ending December 31, 1934.

Date of Marriage / Place of Marriage	Name and Name of Groom and Bride / Residence of Each at Time of Marriage	Age in Years	Color / No.	Times Married	Place of Birth of Groom and Bride / Occupation of Each at the time of Marriage	Name of Father / Maiden Name of Mother	Place of Birth of Parents	Occupation	Name, Official Station and Residence of Person by whom Married
Feb. 7 Bartlett N. H.	Ethan Hersey	21		1	Burke, Maine Laborer	Forrest Hersey Edith Hurd	G. Tuftonboro Berwick, Maine	Farmer Housewife	Robert E. Jones Clergyman Bartlett, N. H.
	Lillian Burke	19		1	Bartlett, N. H. At Home	Joseph Burke Alice Wd	Bartlett	R.R.S.Man Housewife	
Feb. 23 Brookline Mass.	Walter Roy Smith	26		1	Farmington, N. H. Laborer	James W. Smith Abbie L. Smith	Lowell, Mass. Barrington, N. S.	Laborer Housekeeper	Crawford O. Smith Clergyman Brookline, Mass.
	Cora Emma Stillings	25		1	Ossipee, N. H. At Home	Frank O. Stillings Kate M. Stillings	Alton, N. H. Tuftonboro	Farmer Wife	
de 30 Tuftonboro	Arnold LeRoy Ridlon	20		1	Wolfeboro, N. H. Shoe Worker	Arthur LeRoy Ridlon Lena G. Shannon	Tuftonboro Gloucester, Mass.	Carpenter Wife	John E. MacMartin Clergyman Wolfeboro, N. H.
	Anna Estelle Powers	18	III White	1	At Wife	William Chs. Powers Alice Margar. Meuse	Yarmouth, N. S.	Laborer Laundry W.	
Sept. 6 Wolfeboro N. H.	Donald Joseph Mugridge	28		1	Prince Edw. Isl. Can. Mechanic	Thomas J. Mugridge Annie Gillis	Prince Edw. Isl. N.S. " " "	Carpenter At Home	Orman T. Headley Minister Wolfeboro, N. H.
	Eleanor Pearl Howe	19		1	Attleboro, Mass. Waitress	Carlton L. Howe Ina Maud Cordeau	Southboro, Ms. Marlboro, Mass.	Carpenter Housewife	
Ot. 3 Wol Bbo N. H.	Ivan Es Piper	23		1	Wolfeboro, N. H. Farmer	Ivan J. Piper Winnifred Allard	Wolfeboro, N. H. Eaton, " "	Farmer Housewife	Orma T. Headley Minister Bbo, N. H.
	Eleanor Josephine Morris	22		1	Melvin Village Waitress	Frederick J. Morris Hattie J. Buzzell	Biddeford, Me. Meredith, N. H.	Retired Housewife	
Dec. 6 Center Oss- ipe, N. H.	Charles Wesley Nancy	26		1	Boston, Mass. Laborer	Hnry A. Wo Nancy Florence I. Evans	Roslindale, Ms. Boston, Mass.	Retired Housewife	Fra lnH. Baker Mh' ter of the Gospel Ossipee, N. H.
	Eleanor May Thompson	17		1	Tuftonboro	Simon T. Thompson Evelyn L. Bean	Tuftonboro Tuftonboro	Farmer Housewife	

I hereby etify that the above return is correct, erding to the best of my k nw edge and belief.

MARION L. NER, Town Clerk.

Births Registered in the Town of Tuftonboro, N. H., for the year ending December 31, 1934.

Date and Birthplace of Child	Name of Child	Sex	Living – Stillborn	No. of Child	Color	Name of Father / Maiden Name of Mother	Age in Years	Color of Parents	Occupation of Father / Residence of Parents	Birthplace of Father / Birthplace of Mother
April 13 Wolfeboro	Joan Marilyn Forsythe	F	L	2	All White	Frank F. Forsythe, Jr. / Gladys Viola Spidel	31 / 26	All White	Farming / Housewife, Ctr. Tuftonboro	Lynn, Mass. / Lexington, Mass.
April 27 Wolfeboro	Virginia May Hopkinson	F	L	10		Thomas Hopkinson / Sarah E. Jose	50 / 38		Farmer / Housewife, Mirror Lake	England / Saco, Maine
June 23 Wolfeboro	Greydon Herbert Hodgdon	M	L	2		Forrest W. Hodgdon / Frances Canning	33 / 28		Asst. Foreman / Housewife, Tuftonboro	Cambridge, Mass. / Stowe, Vt.
July 2 Tuftonboro	Joan May Stead	F	L	2		Harold L. Stead / Thelma May Shannon	21 / 20		Farmer / Housewife, Mirror Lake	Boston, Mass. / So. Wolfeboro
Oct. 2 Wolfeboro	Richard Leon Dore	M	L	4		Leon E. Dore / Mildred F. Davis	39 / 27		Farmer / Housewife, Ctr. Tuftonboro	Ossipee, N. H. / Tuftonboro
Oct. 9 Tuftonboro	Forrest Creighton Rudolph	M	L	3		Roy Rudolph / Julia May Roghaar	36 / 32		Farmer / Housewife, Tuftonboro	Canada / Lynn, Mass.
Oct. 19 Tuftonboro	Barbara Jeanne Eldridge	F	L	6		Carlton S. Eldridge / Esther M. Haley	32 / 29		Farmer / Housewife, Tuftonboro	Ossipee, N. H. / Tuftonboro
Nov. 24 Wolfeboro	Robert Maurice Mack	M	L	1		Maurice J. Mack / Christine Elliott	23 / 24		Laborer / Housewife, Ctr. Tuftonboro	Laconia, N. H. / Alton, N. H.
Dec. 10 Wolfeboro	Marjorie Ann Brown	F	L	3		George H. Brown / Nellie Morris	33 / 32		Farmer / Housewife, Ctr. Tuftonboro	Campton, N. H. / England

I hereby certify that the above return is correct, according to the best of my knowledge and belief.

MARION L. HORNER, Town Clerk.

Date and Place of Death	Name, Surname and Birthplace of Deceased	Age Years	Age Months	Age Days	Sex	Color	Single, Married or Widowed	Occupation	Father	Birthplace and Name of Mother Maiden Name
July 12 Mirror Lake	George Anderson Loring Hingham, Mass.	77	1	5	M	All White	M	Retired	Enos Loring Hingham, Mass.	- - - Hingham, Mass.
July 23 Ctr. Tuftonboro	Mary E. McInnis - - - -	68	0	19	F		W		George Chase Portsmouth, N. H.	Unknown New Hampshire
Dec. 11 Laconia, N. H.	Juliette Ladd Tamworth, N. H.	77	11	10	F		M	Housewife	James Bickford Madbury, N. H.	Sarah J. Tilton Tamworth, N. H.
Dec. 18 Tuftonboro	Frances S. Thompson Somersworth, N. H.	100	0	4	F		W	At Home	George Kenison Newton, N. H.	Lizia N. Peavey Farmington, N. H.

I hereby certify that the above return is correct, according to the best of my knowledge and belief.

MARION L. HORNER, Town Clerk.

Lightning Source UK Ltd.
Milton Keynes UK
UKHW010758221218

334411UK00004B/214/P